The Loneliness
of the
Long-Distance
Gunner

Patrick Mangan

First published in Australia in 2017

by Patrick Mangan

Copyright © Patrick Mangan 2017

ISBN 978-0-9945073-2-7

Cover design by Alicia Freile, Tango Media Pty Ltd

Cover images: landscape by iStock.com/Totajla; football by iStock.com/plastique2; kangaroo icon by iStock.com/ MrsWilkins

Cataloguing-in-Publication entry is available from the National Library of Australia

http://catalogue.nla.gov.au/

Originally published as *Offsider* by Melbourne University Press

Contents

To Mum, Dad, John and Anne

Preface

I'd looked in the mirror a few times before deciding I could almost get away with it. Australia v Iran, 29 November 1997 – a sudden-death World Cup qualification match – was my first major assignment at *The Sunday Age*, and naturally I wanted to present a particular image: something low-key but upmarket, a quietly assured, vertically mobile football writer for the late millennium. Conversely, though, I really, *really* wanted to wear the Socceroos shirt I'd just been given. Which happened to be two, maybe three, sizes too big.

The fashion of the times gave me some leeway, but nowhere near enough. Baggy was one thing, but on my dolphin shoulders a shiny green Socceroos sack, adorned with a Soccer Australia badge the size of a chest plate, would always fail to flatter. I'd made my decision, though, and I'd wear it, cutting a distinctive, if not dashing, figure in the media throng of sober monochrome shirts, ties and T-shirts.

I was on the phone to the sports desk at the paper when the Socceroos scored their second goal. The media area at the Melbourne Cricket Ground erupted like kids on break-up day, a classroom of whoops and thrashing arms, and I had to pull the receiver away from my ear as Rohan Connolly, the acting sports editor, celebrated with a guttural holler. Forty-eight minutes gone: Australia 2, Iran 0.

'There's your story,' Rohan bellowed down the line. '"Australia qualifies for the World Cup finals" …'

'Yeah?' I wondered out loud.

'Yeah,' he confirmed.

Okay, so he was tempting fate, but we were on a tight deadline. *They can't print the second edition of the paper till you've finished your match report.* I'd mulled it over a little, tossed it about a bit, pondered it once or twice as I sauntered, sweating profusely, around town during the week: how do you simultaneously watch a soccer game *and* write a punchy 500 words packed with incisive adjectives and acute observations, submitting it within ten minutes of the final whistle? The adjectives and observations might be an early casualty, but I felt I could just about manage a few hundred words as long as nothing – nothing at all – peculiar happened to throw the story off kilter. A mind-numbing 0–0 draw would be perfect.

Even with a scoreless dirge, though, the pressure would be on. I'd been the soccer writer for the newspaper for about six weeks and my match reports of South Melbourne v Gippsland Falcons and Carlton v Perth

Glory in the national soccer league, buried so deep in the sports section they'd almost come out the back of the TV guide, had been read by literally dozens of people. And now they were holding the presses for me. I was kind of apprehensive.

Back in my seat, with a Stalag of floodlights, 85,000 people and a soccer match testing my peripheral vision, I stared at the computer screen. Due to demand on the day, I was using one of *The Age*'s back-up laptops, evidently a 1970s model – I think I'd seen them on *The Curiosity Show*.[1] You could only read five or six lines of text at a time and the cursor was slower than the Iranian defence, but it did the job: or, rather, would have done, if my fingers hadn't been paralysed at the keyboard.

Maybe I was trying too hard. After all, the Socceroos' periodic tilt at the World Cup – five desperate, tragicomic attempts since 1974 – had become one of the most compelling (in a drunk-on-a-precipice sort of way) stories of Australian sport. The 3–0 or 4–0 hammering of Iran that was set to banish a generation of failure demanded an epic turn of phrase, but I was struggling to nail it. I was gazing at an unfinished sentence spilling off the tiny screen – 'Nineteen-year-old Harry Kewell opened the scoring, his far-post finish leaving the Iranian keeper …' – when someone noticed a ruckus behind one of the goals. The entire room squinted to see a net dangling off one of the crossbars, a startled Persian goalkeeper, and a spectator being escorted from the ground by police. Strange.

It was a few minutes before the match could restart. Interesting footnote, I thought, I'll have to squeeze a line or two about that somewhere into the tale of triumph. But back to the game and just over half an hour left. I was watching history unfold: writer's block or not, this was going to be great.

Part I

Murtoa and I

Mark Twain had a good eye for this sort of thing. On an antipodean tour in 1895, in which he enlightened the wheat-encrusted citizens of the Wimmera with his Morals lecture, the author noted the stark terrain that lapped against the carriage as he approached Horsham station: 'gray, bare, sombre', he'd etched in his journal, 'melancholy, baked, cracked …'

Eighty years on, as I looked around the grass-shy park that bordered St Brigid's College, a few weary, out-of-season locusts failing to obscure the flan-flat vista, it was clear you couldn't rightly argue. Assuming that in half a lifetime in Australia you'd paid the slightest attention to the landscape; melancholy, baked, braised or otherwise. This eleven-year-old hadn't been so easily distracted.

Mr Twain, among others, may have found the Wimmera an intriguing, intimidating place – an hour up the road was Lake Albacutya, its lonely jetty and stern boating regulations superfluous for the nine years each decade it was nothing but hectares of rasping sand. To be honest, though, the Wimmera had never quite held my interest. And today less than usual; for today I was Brian Kidd.

Brian was one of the stars of the worst Arsenal team in half a century. In a Gunners line-up seemingly destined to effect the club's first relegation since 1913, he'd somehow finished second top scorer in the whole division. It was a feat miraculous enough to book a permanent place for the man in my affections, whether or not I took a shine to the towering perm that nearly swallowed his head. For the record, I thought it was pretty cool.

Coughlan Park seemed weirdly adrift in an Aussie Rules football town; untouched, like a prize rose garden, most of the year. With just a hundred or so boys at our school there was only the occasional lacklustre kick-to-kick in a corner of the oval, while an alluring expanse was left open for an alternative if, say, a few kids stumbled upon a scuffed-grey soccer ball in a gym cupboard.

I was pretty sure there were fewer than half-a-dozen soccer balls within the Wimmera education system, so this was big. A bunch of other Year 7s had decided it might be alright to boot it around for a while and to my amazement – in a school where, image-wise, soccer was right up there with chicken pox – I spent idyllic lunchtimes toe-poking a faded, peeled ball across Coughlan Park, luxuriating under the weight of

Brian Kidd's locks. March was a beautiful, spherical, blue-skied month. Then in stepped Dick Dwan.

As Dick and three of his stringy-haired Year 11 classmates stomped into the midst of our kickabout one day, there were cigarettes hanging precariously from their lips as they passed around the Jack Daniel's. Or maybe it was musk sticks[2] and a bottle of Marchants.[3] Effectively grown men among children, Dick's crew sauntered about school with an air of violence yet to be unleashed wafting around them. A Chinese burn could easily be on the agenda.

In the age of *Welcome Back, Kotter* they could all do Vinnie Barbarino in a bad mood, and when they asked if we'd like to take them on – at soccer, fortunately – we, Horshacks of Horsham, knew it was an offer we couldn't refuse. They lined up in their half of the small pitch – four of them, about twelve of us; aggregate heights roughly the same either side of the halfway line – and the battle commenced.

Against the odds it proved to be an even, if surreal, contest – a plague of insects swatted at by a cluster of thick-skinned, lumbering beasts, with a soccer ball buried in there somewhere. For my part I took a while to settle. In the first week I was on edge, rarely venturing within cooee of the green-jumper goalposts defended by redwood legs, with size 12 school shoes in too-short trousers hacking clearances all the way back to our goalkeeper at the other end. It looked dangerous up there.

After a few days, though, with no significant casualties recorded, I realised Dick and his mates probably weren't out for blood, as such. Arguably they had little to gain by maiming a fellow pupil: this wasn't *Lord of the Flies*, we had nuns here. Despite the good news, I didn't quite see myself launching into a full-bodied challenge with a Year 11 whose navel was in the same horizontal plane as my chin.

It had been a critical few weeks. For one thing Arsenal had somehow belted West Ham 6–1 to more or less stave off relegation again. Dreams of emulating glamour teams like Derby County (reigning champions) or Queen's Park Rangers (currently second) were clearly absurd, but … 6–1!!! Unless a criminally negligent sub-editor at *The Age* had let an errant 6 slip through rather than the overwhelmingly more likely 0 (and I relied on these people more than my parents; in the usual absence of match reports in the papers, or any mention whatsoever on TV sports round-ups, the classified scores on the Monday were what you'd cling to), I had reason to believe we'd rocketed from seventeenth to thirteenth on the ladder. Relegation might have to wait until 1977.

The Gunners aside, I'd just begun secondary school at St Brigid's; no particular drama, as such, in the Catholic stream of a country town where the same couple of hundred kids hounded each other throughout the dozen years or less of their education. I'd been daunted, though, by the prospect of sharing a corridor with platoons of teenagers with Lillee-ish wisps on their upper lip, and had I known that a boy in Year 9, Tim Watson, would combine next year's studies with playing senior VFL[4] football for Essendon, I might never have been coaxed out of bed on the first morning.

But at a time when life was pointing me, irretrievably I hoped, towards manhood, there were equal and opposite forces at work. In the week I started at St Brigid's, I also, with a spectacular sense of folly, embarked on a course of piano lessons. Like a dumb kid, like Mel Gibson's reckless mate in *Gallipoli*, I'd run full tilt to the recruitment officers, thinking it wouldn't do any harm to learn to hammer out a tune or two on the old Joanna. I'd failed to allow for the dag factor. The piano? What was I thinking?

From the initial trip to Mrs Schirmer's home it was clear this had to be a covert operation. I suspected as much from the moment she sat me down on a piano stool hopelessly too high for my spindly legs and, smiling jauntily, said, 'Let me introduce you to Jibbidy-F and A-C-E.' I shuddered, instinctively reading her *Play School* tone. I could tell this wasn't some weird, hip musical terminology like, say, 'Magneto and Titanium Man', a song by Wings in my elder brother John's tape collection, and I didn't think I'd be rushing to brag to the Year 11s about old Jibbidy-F. I was right.

Propping a music book on the wooden ledge, Mrs

Schirmer pointed with rare enthusiasm at two cartoon figures on its washed-out front cover. 'This is Jibbidy-F': she drove an index finger into the shallow stomach of the slightly chirpier one. 'He represents the notes on the top four lines of the treble clef – G, B, D, F. If you say them quickly it sounds like Jibbidy-F,' she said. My jaw dropped, but she was – fair's fair – spot on.

A-C-E were the notes in between, she added, but my mind was already elsewhere. The rest of the lesson was a bit of a blur, the just-revealed landscape of Jibbidy-F and A-C-E an appalling thing for a Year 7 to take on board. The potential psychological impact on John (age: thirteen) – waiting in the lounge room for his first lesson, oblivious to his fate – can only be imagined. But I knew, looking across at him as we walked up our driveway in Federation Avenue that evening: there and then John and I made a silent pact never, ever, to speak of what had passed between us at Mrs Schirmer's.

To add insult to possible injury we didn't have a piano at home, so the only practice I could do was at school. And I had a particular dread of my music activities being uncovered by – for instance – Dick Dwan, who, as I saw it, was unlikely to be impressed by the leprechaun netherworld of piano lessons. So I smuggled *Jibbidy-F* into the building past heavily armed checkpoints, hidden among geography, history and German textbooks, nervously anticipating how the conversation might pan out should Dick find the incriminating evidence (I never got much beyond 'Dick … um … you're hurting me'). Happily, as summer blurred into autumn, he hadn't been gripped by an inexplicable urge to rifle through my belongings: our only head-to-head battle would come on the field.

I'm not sure of the machinations involved, whether or not a teacher or two had witnessed the squadron of Year 7s tackling the Dick Dwan quartet, but within weeks a funny thing happened: probably the first soccer fixture in St Brigid's history was pencilled in. Usually, a sporting contest would pit us against our arch-rivals at Horsham High or Tech. It may not have been a ringing endorsement of the football prowess on view that, instead, we were heading to Murtoa. A recently erected signpost at Horsham's city limits proudly declared our number at 11,100 and rising. Murtoa, 25 miles north-east with barely a thousand inhabitants, was a speck on the map in comparison. If our skills were a tad rudimentary, what could a Murtoa High soccer XI possibly unleash upon us?

A junior and a senior game were scheduled, and as one of the most diminutive students yet admitted to an Australian secondary school, I was a natural candidate for the younger line-up. So it proved, but when the teams were posted a few days later, half-buried amid a crowded notice board, I shivered as I came to the dismal realisation: there was the word 'capt.' beside my name. Oh God, I was going to be in charge.

Presumably, my being the only kid in Year 7 or 8 who'd recognise a flat back four in a back paddock had led to me getting the armband. Somehow my pathological shyness hadn't deterred the St Brigid's powers-that-be. I'd scored a 'very good' for English on a recent report card, with just the tiny proviso: 'does not join in oral expression unless forced to. He is sometimes unable to talk on a simple topic.' As far as I could tell, leading Catholic troops into battle in pagan outposts seemed dangerously low on my list of natural talents.

The bus trip to Murtoa was tense. We were placed in the hands of the ubiquitous Krahe company (official Horsham pronunciation – 'kray') and their usual driver with slicked, short back and sides and glued-on sunnies, a man never caught smiling in an entire career at the wheel. Inevitably, his nickname was Crabby Krahe. As I climbed the steps of the bus with *Krahe* on the side, the letters angled sharply like we'd get to Murtoa at jet-engine speed, the wink of encouragement I hadn't anticipated didn't materialise.

Both St Brigid's teams were on board, and as the juggernaut rolled through featureless dry scrub down the narrow, chipped-asphalt road, John and his senior team mates joked with each other like kids on a pleasant school outing. Towards the back, looking out a smudged window at rosellas, cockatoos and miles of red-gum fence-posts, I chewed at stubs of fingernails, frustrated by the holiday-camp atmosphere, nervous. 'Come on,' I whispered to myself and my comrades, 'this isn't *fun*, this is *soccer*.'

Crabby Krahe cranked the bus past the willow-tree-bordered lake that lent brutal Murtoa a deceptively genteel veneer and deposited us deep within the high school on the outskirts of town. John and his friends sauntered lazily past the deathly expressionless driver and onto dusty foreign soil, while I took a breath, picked my soccer boots up from the floor and quietly pondered my fate.

The jewel in Murtoa's crown was a grain storage complex bordering the school grounds, a skyscraper in the spirit-level flatness. Essentially a massive shed a city-block long with adjoining tubes and other metal contraptions, suspended five or six storeys above the ground and surrounded by silos, it was the sort of structure a casual observer might have found diverting. But as a few of us took a walk around the school I was so intent on the task ahead, head down and brow furrowed to the bone, that the slightly rusted *Jetsons* space station to my immediate left didn't even register.

Pele was inclined to call soccer *'o jogo bonito'* – the beautiful game – but St Brigid's v Murtoa High was no oil painting. It was all cracked clay and granite-toed footy boots, a bruising encounter that might as well have been decided by touchdowns; and I amazed myself by loving it. As I shook hands with a burly Murtoa captain seemingly old enough to vote, I realised I desperately needed to bluff. Myself first, then maybe the rest of the team. It was a bizarre revelation, that if I acted like I was the boss it was possible I would be. Staggeringly it kind of worked and from time to time during the ninety minutes I ignored my actual personality, politely shouting instructions to team mates, marvelling at the anomaly of hearing my raised voice out in the open air. Like someone else was at the controls I made some vigorous, captain-like runs from midfield, as well as the usual handful of soccerish touches and passes, almost feeling that these ten other kids were occasionally looking to me for guidance. And, incredibly, that I might be able to provide it.

Naturally we were hammered, 4–1. The Murtoa team was primed for the contest and with their beef-eating bulk we were hopelessly undermanned. In the shadow of the Empire State silos, though, I'd felt the power seeping through my untanned torso in the midst of a match we never looked like winning.

There were no two ways about it: a three-goal defeat was ugly. But there was dignity as the dirt whirlpool of the previous hour and a half began to settle in slow waves, and, proud in the knowledge that we'd survived in a manly fashion, we walked handsomely from the park despite the loss. I could even begin to contemplate the world outside – like the rusted Vicrail grain carriages and dull-orange railway tracks running alongside the storage complex only yards from the touchline – as I finally lifted my head.

The adrenaline pulsing, still clad for battle in our rib-tight green T-shirts, we strode the 100 yards to the other oval to watch the senior game. It was crude too, a bludgeoning match between a bunch of kids whose minds seemed elsewhere, and we won easily enough, 3–0. I congratulated John and his team mates and was greeted with the unspoken big-smoke bravado of 'Of course we beat Murtoa High. We're from *Horsham*.'

The school bus ambled home towards a broad red sunset, taking in again a dry sea of paddocks and eucalypts peeling bark like burned skin. Crabby Krahe was deadpan at the wheel, like everyone else acting as if nothing had altered. Like I hadn't captained St Brigid's juniors as a real captain. Like Arsenal hadn't just scored six goals in a match to more or less stave off relegation till 1977. Like the world was standing still.

But if it was all moving too quickly to take in, reality was kind enough to set me straight. When we got home, the story I told Mum and Dad and my younger sister, Anne, seemed strangely unfulfilled with the tag line of a 4–1 shellacking, especially in the light of the seniors' imperious result. And to rub it in, by the end of the week the Gunners had been thrashed 3–0 by Leeds United and were slipping perilously back down the table. That's if you believed the soccer results section of *The Age*.

A Whim and a Prayer

If the English daredevil Donald Campbell had been the musical type, it might have consoled him that just hours away from his desert limbo four of his countrymen were drumming up as loud a storm as South Australia had ever heard. A quarter of a million fans – the biggest crowd ever to greet the Beatles – flooded the balconies and strained vantage points of Adelaide airport as the band flew in from Hong Kong.

Four specks of shaggy-haired black disappeared into a matchbox-sized limousine, while Campbell, at the heart of a million-pound attempt on the world land speed record, his 3-ton iron beast lying under a tarpaulin in the South Australian desert, watched another twelve-hours' daylight blow uselessly away as the wind refused to drop for a test run. With money streaming down a drizzly, gusty drain, in the second week of June 1964 Campbell seemed at least as annoyed that he couldn't even 'get a decent onion around here'. This was a harsh country.

As Donald and the Beatles were tackling a cultural and actual wasteland on the far side of the planet, a fellow Englishman was being born in a semi-detached brick house in the north London suburb of Southgate. Conveniently, it was me.

My parents, both of Irish descent, lived in Chase Road, where a sprinkling of Celtic and Jewish families lent the place a moderately cosmopolitan air. Nonetheless, there was authentic ethnic Englishness within reach. There was football, for starters, and conversations about Dad's chance encounter with Spurs captain Danny Blanchflower on the Underground, or Stanley Matthews' decision to retire after barely 750 games, occasionally filled our sitting room, colliding with the sound of Herman's Hermits, Gilbert & Sullivan and Tchaikovsky on our chunky brown hi-fi. And impressively, Grandad – on my father's side – could lay claim to a scrap of genuine British football history, albeit against his better judgement at the time.

The 1923 FA Cup final marked the opening of Wembley Stadium, one of the biggest sporting arenas in the world, and Grandad had headed across London for the match. As he neared the ground, though, he realised a couple of hundred thousand other folk had had the same idea, and thought for safety's sake an afternoon of gardening might be a better bet. Resistance was useless, however, and Grandad was swept along in an army of trilbies and flat caps, past the gates left open resignedly by fretful ground staff. Though the recorded crowd was 126,947, Grandad became an unofficial, involuntary statistic among the 200,000-plus spectators who witnessed – to varying degrees – the first-ever match at Wembley. Bolton beat West Ham 2–0, but the gallant attempts of PC George Scorey and his white horse, Billie, to clear the crowd from the edge of the pitch became more famous than the result. Thousands of fans watched the game only inches from the touchline, and legend has it that one throw-in was taken by a spectator.

Grandad made it home intact, satisfied enough by his day out and unfussed by the result, being a fan of Tottenham Hotspur. Had he known, he might have been more perturbed to discover that the supporting of Spurs would not only elude his eldest son, Shawn, two years old at the time of the Wembley assembly, but every other male in his family over the course of the next eight decades. This serial disloyalty didn't seem to leave too deep a scar; it didn't, at least, take years off his life. He reached the age of ninety-one, still waiting in vain for an inkling of football solidarity from among his flesh and blood.

Although Grandad failed to steer his offspring in the direction of Spurs – whose stadium was only a brisk walk from their home in Enfield – three of his sons became soccer fans in rapid succession in the late 1920s. Shawn decided to barrack for Arsenal, the second-closest of the 90-odd clubs in the country. Kevin, next in line, enigmatically claimed Aston Villa (home ground Villa Park, Birmingham; about 100 miles from the nearest bus stop), while our dad plumped for the Gunners as well. My father's younger brother, Den, later to become a Catholic priest and live in Rhodesia, decided it might be healthier to abstain.

By the 1960s, Dad was working as an eye doctor at the Western Ophthalmic Hospital near Madame Tussaud's waxworks in the middle of London. He'd see a conveyor belt of patients during any given week and never lay eyes on them again. Slightly dispirited, and not relishing being tethered to the National Health Service for the term of his natural life, he was intrigued to receive a letter from a doctor friend, offering him a job up the road from his friend's own practice. There was just the one hitch: Dr Gorman lived in Bendigo, Australia.

It could have been worse. Bendigo, a lively town of 30,000 inhabitants, was a bare two or three hours drive north of Melbourne, admittedly one of the southern-most cities on Earth. Ominously, though, the practice in question was in Swan Hill, population 8000 and another 120 miles inland, a couple of hours further from Melbourne, a couple of hours closer to Australia's desert core. To pep things up, Dr Gorman added that if he didn't hear from us within a month, he'd advertise the job in the *British Medical Journal*. Given Dad's dissatisfaction at work he decided it was worth a look, no matter how preposterous moving to the Southern Hemisphere might seem. My parents set out for Australia House.

In 1969 the Australian government was at the tail end of a crusade to pump appropriately vetted foreigners onto its fertile plains, at least partly to quell the Communist peril from the north. The 'White Australia' immigration policy had been relaxed in the aftermath of World War II when, with its compelling 'Populate Or Perish' slogan, the government decided a dash of Mediterraneans, Balkans and others couldn't do too much harm. There were also the '10-pound tourists', a scheme introduced in the 1950s in which approved applicants were charged the princely sum of a tenner to migrate. The only catch was having to stay in Australia at least two years, otherwise you were retrospectively billed in full for your trip.

At Australia House, in the heart of the Strand, the mood was casually upbeat. The phrase on colour posters and on the lips of everyone in the old building was that just £10 away was a country for 'Excelling Yourself Every Day'. This was good news, but the unsolicited remark of a passer-by made a deeper impression. Dad was perusing a carousel of blindingly blue-skied brochures when an Australian woman sidled up and, with the trademark nasal drawl, offered a piece of grave advice. 'If you're a no-hoper here,' she said slowly, 'you're a no-hoper there.'

Unsettlingly, no-one at Australia House seemed

even to have heard of Swan Hill. 1960s England was neither the time nor the place for researching obscure villages down under, but against the odds a trip to the library in Enfield unlocked the town's most potent secret. It was there Dad made the remarkable discovery that Swan Hill had an annual Shakespearean festival – a crucial piece of evidence. So with a gentle push from the Bard (how bad could a place be if it had Shakespeare on board?), as my parents reflected on their prospects in a neatly green, thoroughly civilised suburb of north London, they grew more and more convinced that transplanting their family to the other end of the planet was an excellent option.

Telling their parents and others of their crazy plan must have been daunting, not least for Dad, a quiet man for whom some might have assumed that, expedition-wise, the occasional round at Whitewebbs Golf Club and an annual holiday in county Kerry had him stretched. Then there was the awkward task of informing the kids: Mum and Dad tackled it head-on. We were given a picture book about Australia – brimming with delicately undulating, water-colour scenery, cute snuffly marsupials and lightly tanned, grinning Anglo faces – and Mum asked hopefully, 'Wouldn't it be marvellous if we could go there for a holiday?' We said 'Super!' setting in motion a subtle, gradual process whereby she eventually mentioned how brilliant it would be to go to Australia and never,

ever come back – if I'm remembering correctly.

For me and John, who were almost lackadaisical about this migration business but pretty keen on cars, the turning point came when we saw a photo spread in *Motor* magazine featuring a Holden Brougham. We'd never spotted these Aussie machines anywhere near north London and they seemed remotely, hopelessly glamorous, like Disneyland or Tarzan. 'It'd be terrific to see a Brougham,' I said to John, perhaps undermining my suavity by pronouncing it 'Broffem'. We quickly committed ourselves to the move. Neil Armstrong landed on the moon and John and I watched the footage on the BBC news as we contemplated our own journey into the outer atmosphere.

In the last few days, as relatives came over from Ireland and around England to say goodbye, I noticed for the first time the regret in the air: I hadn't imagined that people other than the five of us might be affected, and Mum and Dad had been relentlessly enthusiastic. It was clear, though, how emotional my grandparents were at our disappearance from their lives. 'We're delighted we're going to Australia,' I told them seriously the evening before we left, 'but we're sorry we're leaving you.'

It was an uncharacteristic slip into empathy and, sadly, on the day itself I was truer to form. Grandad came to Chase Road to see us off, one last look at us all, and after we'd packed everything we could into our

Vauxhall Victor estate car, Dad started the engine. The three children tumbled across the back seat and amid a silently traumatic farewell scene – for the grown-ups, anyway – I closed the door, smiled at Grandad and ventured a cheery, carefree 'Bye, bye!'

New York, San Francisco, Honolulu, Fiji: it was a viable, if marathon, route and a 34-hour cultural explosion for a child. Never mind the heartbreak my parents were experiencing, at hip-height I was in paradise. Just the transit lounges were enough, packed with palm trees, complimentary sugar cubes and a river of American voices through PAs and in the open air, while an eight-door Cadillac on the tarmac at Honolulu kept John and me engaged in rigorous discussion as our Boeing 707 chugged closer to Australia.

After a final stopover in Sydney we landed mid-afternoon at Essendon Airport in Melbourne, met by Dr Gorman and his wife. They smiled broadly and bundled us into their Volkswagen estate, set to bury us all deep in the Victorian wilderness. As we drove through Melbourne the car filled with the sharp edge of Australian accents, and I grimly concluded that everyone in this country probably talked like the Gormans. Equally disorienting was the discovery that an estate car was known as a *station wagon* here; how could there be different words for the same thing? Ten minutes from Essendon Airport, Australia had begun to unnerve me.

There were a couple of distractions as the Calder

Highway took us through Diggers Rest and on towards central Victoria: bony gum trees, the red-and-white splash of nameless exotic birds, and undiscovered Ford Fairmonts, Valiant Regals and, happily, Holden Broffems in the oncoming traffic. There was also the cold. We'd heard the Mallee enjoyed a balmy 65°F average in September, but as we motored along with the sun about to set, the sting had gone from the day, and, in any case, we were still 150 miles from the Mallee – on the Douglas Mawson side. Regrettably, the family wardrobe – a cargo of five suitcases; a glut of T-shirts, shorts and modest English-style swimwear – didn't allow much leeway.

Twelve months later Mum recorded a reel-to-reel tape for her brother across the globe, with a note in passing about 'cold, wet, miserable, horrible Bendigo'. It was there we spent the night at the Gormans', in a house full of wooden rooms and loud children, and in a time-zone semi-coma Mum and Dad washed and dressed for bed, preparing to take their family to a town called Swan Hill they'd never laid eyes on. I wonder how often they'd rolled the word around in their mouths – 'home'. Go to a place with a yawning 12,000-mile crater separating yourself from everyone you've ever known. Drag your three jet-lagged children along with you and call a house and a street home, without even knowing how to light the gas heater in your lounge room. Simple.

Life on Mars?

Maybe shell-shocked after two centuries of white settlement, the spirits of the land looked upon a deserted road, silent but for a couple of Volkswagens grinding slowly north, one a Beetle nearly anchored to the asphalt with cheap suitcases; inside, a pallid family shivering in their casual summer best still three months from the actual season. You could almost hear the ghostly chuckle at the latest arrival on their shores.

After Mass at Bendigo cathedral on the Sunday morning we set off with the Gormans again, this time spread over two cars, one of which they were kindly lending us till we could organise a vehicle for ourselves. The trip to Swan Hill was an eye-opener: 120 miles through wasted land, alternating between swamps and near-desert, punctuated with avenues of ratty, sucked-dry trees. Now and again our Volkswagen-train closed in on what looked, from a distance, like a stray skyscraper. It'd turn out to be a wheat silo four storeys high, maybe surrounded by a railway track, a flat-roofed weatherboard house or two and signposts to a local cemetery, all speckled with washed-out tufts of grass. Elsewhere there might be a couple of moth-eaten palm trees, swathes of spectral eucalypts and the occasional warning of 'Kangaroos next 10 miles', but otherwise there were no homes, no people, no cars. What on earth were we getting ourselves into?

After two hours of desolation we seemed – briefly – to have arrived at the Paris end of the Mallee. The outskirts of Swan Hill were green and neat, and with a glimpse of the sun and real people strolling across actual lawn, we were very nearly cautiously optimistic, a long, long twenty-four hours since we'd touched down in Essendon. But as we drove slowly – like tourists, ironically; we were *locals* now – towards Mulbar Street a few blocks away, the atmosphere again took on a barren edge. Dad eased the Beetle into the driveway of our Housing Commission house in a street of forty or so identikit residences. Wading through the unruly, weed-strewn front garden, we struggled inside the front door and let it sink in.

You couldn't say it didn't bear a certain resemblance to the semi-detached brick house we'd left behind in London, what with it having four walls and a roof and such. Even to one of the world's less observant five-year-olds, however, the differences were more striking. It was a simple square structure with sheet-thin walls and boarding-house wallpaper, a few beds, a kitchen table and chairs, a settee, a little gas heater in the sitting room; that was about it. Compared to our Chase Road fortress the house seemed unnervingly frail, like you might kick a hole in it if you didn't mind your feet. And the back garden was equally stark: a large patch of bare soil dissected by a concrete path leading to a rotary clothesline, without a tree or shrub in sight. Meanwhile, out the front there was nothing but a letterbox perched on a short, unsteady pole. It was ever so humble. It was no place like home.

After helping with the luggage, the Gormans headed back to Bendigo, leaving us to their Beetle and our own devices. Mum and Dad unpacked the bags, our belongings hardly impinging on the emptiness, while John and I ran our few toy cars along the thinly carpeted floor, the open spaces a perfect blank canvas for our London-to-Sydney Rally and races at Brands Hatch. I didn't let myself think too hard; the idea that we didn't live in England anymore was too odd to get my head around. We had a clutch of Matchbox cars in a shell of a shared bedroom, but none of our books, no Lego, no other toys, no winter clothes; all of that was somewhere off the coast of France inching towards the Southern Hemisphere. Landmarks were in short supply.

The worst thing for my parents had been the fear of isolation, but a knock at the front door signalled an upside to life in Swan Hill. Neighbours dropped by all afternoon to welcome us to town – a disarming

level of friendliness for a handful of wary Londoners
– and, in passing, cheerfully alerted us to the local
demographics. Most families had about five kids, they
said, so that was eighty all-up in Mulbar Street. Clearly,
loneliness, at least in terms of people per square inch,
wouldn't be a worry. At sundown, after hours of
socialising, my parents digested the day's events: this
far into the desert, their first thoughts might have been
of impending claustrophobia.

Monday was the start of a new term at St Mary's
primary school, an excellent time for me and John to
enter the fray. It was a logical proposition and as we
were led, slightly groggy, through the gate, with Mum
depositing John peaceably enough in a room bursting
with seventy-five Grade 2 and 3 kids, a potentially
fraught task wasn't proving too traumatic. But while
my brother exhibited the sang-froid of a six-year-old
James Bond, she'd have no such luck with the younger
of her sons.

Still jet-lagged and disoriented, I was seized
with stage fright as I stood at the classroom door.
Confronted by a sea of sixty curious Australian faces
perched behind splintered wooden desks, I realised
in a moment of abject horror that we'd left England
for good. Mum and Mrs Egan had to drag me, freshly
polished shoes flailing, literally kicking and screaming
into the Grade Prep class, and Mrs Egan restrained me
– her forearms clasped around my midriff – until Mum

made it to the getaway Volkswagen. I made, I have to admit, something of a spectacle of myself.

Perhaps starting me at school the day after we'd arrived was a minor strategic error. Mum was distraught about my obvious – if a tad overstated – anguish, and it failed to ease her conscience regarding our Australian expedition. By week's end the thought was taking shape, as my parents watched the sun set all the way to the horizon in the Mallee's bulbous skies, that if someone snipped the telephone line out of Swan Hill – robbing them of a Christmas $2-a-minute call to England or Ireland – we'd be stranded.

Embarrassingly, given the performance I'd put on first up, school turned out to be okay. Mum and Dad gradually settled in too, adapting stoically to Mulbar Street's communal living as we neared our first Australian summer and Swan Hill opened its windows en masse. For four months of the year we'd try to catch whatever breath of air might be out there in the heat, even if it meant Andy McDonald, a three-year-old from across the street, climbing in through the sitting room window from time to time to say hello. The soundtrack of dogs yelping, cars dryly wrenching through gears, and black-and-white televisions broadcasting Channel 2 or 11 up and down the street, would become as much a feature of an evening meal as the metallic clank of cutlery.

The sounds emerging from people's mouths were even more startling. I'd known things were awry

Patrick Mangan

after a first glance at the signposts in Campbell Street, where in every direction there were towns – Tooleybuc, Woorinen, Nyah, Lake Boga – whose names might have been invented by bad Scrabble players. Nyahs and Bogas rolled off the tongues of kids around me, though, and unfathomably it was *me* who seemed strange to *them*. I hadn't realised my accent veered rather close to the Royal Family – dangerously close – but unaccountably nobody seemed too interested in someone well within heckling distance speaking like Prince Charles. The same couldn't be said for John, who became a kind of cult figure, his classmates lining up around the block to hear him announce how old he was – an unfortunate six and a horf.

However, credit where it's due, the Preps were quick to pounce on other oddities, like any absurd English term for something with a different name in Australia. The list of apparently harmless domestic items is brief, but painful: jumper, singlet, parka, runners, thongs. I'd always known them as pullovers, vests, anoraks, plimsolls and flip-flops. Ridicule was inevitable, and although I'd only get it wrong once per item, it was enough to leave me permanently on edge.

I was adjusting to the dialect – it's *sticky* tape; what's *sella* tape, mate? – but there was so much more to assimilate: air conditioners cut into front windows whirring relentlessly, ant-hill mounds on nature strips riddled with ants the size of Dinky cars, and even trees crazily blossoming pink, and bushes launching satellites of golden spores on breezy days, only emphasising how brown everything else was. Then there were the dust storms, when the sky would darken and howling winds swept off the topsoil of the barren Mallee and Riverina terrain. If you didn't get to the windows quickly enough, you'd be cleaning your house for days. Australia was coming in at us from all angles.

Man had landed on the moon, and having hit the surface, Dad set about expanding his boundaries again. He was the only ophthalmologist for 100 miles and his weeks were now dotted with excursions to treat patients in Kerang, Cohuna and elsewhere. Swan Hill airport was part of the ritual too and Dad, plus instructor, would get behind the controls of a Piper Cherokee to fly to Hay or Hopetoun every fortnight or so, a decent progression from inching on to a packed Piccadilly-line train to the Western Ophthalmic for the rest of his career. It was an impressive discovery that, despite living in a nation where a no-hoper would always be a no-hoper, being a doctor could double up with studying for a pilot's licence. It had been eight months since he'd received the letter from Dr Gorman.

April 1970, and a news item in the Swan Hill *Guardian* took us by surprise: Queen Elizabeth II was coming to town. To Swan Hill. The Queen was coming to Swan Hill. (It took a while to sink in.) I was

amazed, I mean, she wasn't *only* coming to Swan Hill –
Tooleybuc could have been on the itinerary too – but
the fact that I'd never laid eyes on her in the lifetime
in which we'd shared a city, and now she was visiting
my new hometown in, with due respect, the middle of
nowhere, seemed like a sign of … well, something.

Queen fever swept St Mary's; the announcement
of a day off schoolwork clinched the deal. The whole
of the school would head out to the showgrounds to
see her in person and, as there was just the slightest
risk of one of us being required to actually speak to
the Queen, Monsignor McMahon – the most senior
Catholic in Swan Hill – called an assembly to advise us
on the necessary protocol. If she deigned to address
a pupil, he announced, we were to call her 'Your
Majesty'. If she found us sufficiently compelling as
to wish to continue to chat, we'd graduate to 'Your
Highness'. Had she nothing better to do than keep the
conversation alive well past its probable use-by date,
'Ma'am' came into play.

Despite being almost six years old, regal protocol
wasn't my forte and I immediately forgot the lot. On a
bright afternoon there were thousands of us gathered
at the showgrounds to greet the Queen, Prince Philip
and their shiny black Rolls-Royce, and so, I was
relieved to note, there wasn't a ghost of a chance of
a royal chinwag. A couple of fairly dull speeches were
delivered from a podium teeming with flowers, then

a couple more; then something else official may have taken place, or maybe not. I might have been beginning to lose interest by this stage. And that was about it.

Call it a non-event, but somehow it meant something to us. The Queen's visit was like an official seal of approval of the Mallee and, coupled with our having found an actual brick house to move into, we were on more of an even keel now. The place in Thurla Street, 400 yards from our first home, was set in a corner of Swan Hill with two distinguishing features. Firstly, there was a channel at the end of the street as deep as a river that kids said was tremendous for catching yabbies, whatever they might be. Secondly, a few houses around the corner were occupied by Aboriginals. I'd seen black people before – some of them worked on the London Underground – but I'd never lived near any and, keen observer of the human condition as I was becoming, I noticed their gardens were rather messy and you'd sometimes hear drunken yelling from their homes after dark. Strangely, as if we'd been brick-walled apart, I never had a single conversation with an Aboriginal kid.

Hot on the heels of the royal tour, the showground hosted another unmissable event – unsurprisingly, it was the Swan Hill Show. As far as Mallee entertainment went, it was hard to beat, not least because of the dodgem cars. As a child, Mum had loved the dodgems at Puck Fair in Killorglin, an annual festival dating from the sixteenth century in which a male goat was hailed as King Puck and paraded around with a crown on its head. While our local equivalent clearly couldn't compete with that, Mum, perhaps with nostalgia on her mind, deposited me and John behind the wheel of an empty dodgem. Part terrified, part exhilarated, our love of cars was suddenly transported from the lounge room to the Colosseum.

Five minutes later, the lounge room had never looked so good. We were younger and smaller than most of the other kids in the arena, many of whom seemed keen to vent their pent-up hatred of society, which had, judging by their kamikaze tendencies, rendered them fairly close to the edge. We copped a barrage of head-ons and sideswipes before a possibly accidental three-car pile-up in the corner of the ring left me with a broken nose.

I'd jerked forward and my face had smacked the dashboard. Naturally I was stoic, barely screaming with the pain as I came to my senses. The local GP gently attended to me as I simpered manfully, but the lesson was well learned. I wouldn't need reminding of the dangers of life in rural Australia.

The Sweet FA

When my parents announced we were leaving Swan Hill for Horsham after two years, the information came ungarnished. There was no preamble, no pretence that Horsham might be a mesmerising place for a holiday, no illustrated books thrilling to the seven natural wonders of the Wimmera district. We were moving because Dad had been offered a new job and … now go to bed.

A hundred and twenty miles south-west of Swan Hill, Horsham had been founded by Englishman James Darlot in the 1830s. It was bigger than Swan Hill, about 10,000 people, and a few miles closer to Melbourne as we inched back to civilisation. We'd be leaving friends behind, but they were only a Lilliputian two-hour drive away, and as an adventure it was a bit of a fizzer.

Had we stayed in London, we'd have been a couple of hundred yards from the Arsenal squad celebrating its first championship in eighteen years at the White Hart hotel in Chase Road: instead, a Bedford removal truck was heading towards an empty house in Dooen

Road with a railway track beyond its back fence. Not always a real-estate selling point, to me railways meant action, so fifty-carriage goods trains juddering past day and night could only bolster Horsham's credentials.

Mark Twain hadn't been slow to note that the Wimmera was a little on the dry side, but, to be fair, he'd also observed it was 'a horizonless ocean of vivid green grass the day after a rain'. I thought that might be pushing it, but the bull ants certainly seemed less vindictive and the mercury not so inclined to nudge 110, while on the culture front our new friends the McClellands had the *Magical Mystery Tour* album in their collection, the likes of which we'd never heard in the pre-psychedelic Mallee. Nonetheless Horsham remained unashamedly rural and, with it, coarse around the edges. Any place where, for three months a year, walking down the main street in your swimming togs was *de rigueur* was always likely to fall short in the fashion stakes.

While I was all but getting the hang of this Australian lifestyle, England was still home and any news from there was greeted like a birthday cake. Now and again an aerogram would arrive from Grandad outlining the latest family ailments, and Tottenham Hotspur and Arsenal – my father's team – featured like troublesome cousins: 'Your uncle Kevin's not well' or 'Spurs have been disappointing me'. Although I knew precisely nothing about soccer – did Arsenal play in green ... black ... purple? – this intelligence kept us plugged into the UK mains.

As Uncle Kevin recovered and, as my grandfather reported, Arsenal were beaten by Leeds in the FA Cup final, John and I became curious about Dad's club. Exhaustive interrogation revealed the following: their nickname was the Gunners and they'd been formed in the 1800s by workers at a munitions factory – which was called an arsenal and made weapons apparently; our uncle Shawn had been to virtually every match of theirs since the late 1920s; and Arsenal's home ground, Highbury, was only a few miles from Chase Road and the three bedrooms I still thought of as our real home. As the evidence mounted it became clear Arsenal FC were an inextricable link with our English past, part of the heart of me I could feel being diluted in the Australian outback. John and his eight-year-old brother were sold.

Seeing the Queen from a telescopic distance had really been rather good, but Her Majesty was about to be topped: we were off to England and Ireland on holiday. My little sister Anne, who couldn't remember much about the UK, took the bulletin on board like a day trip to Warracknabeal, but John and I were bouncing off the walls. It had been three years since we'd migrated – more than a third of my life – and England almost felt like Narnia now. Given how remote it was, in my

memories and elsewhere, the letters from Grandad with
the Queen's head and the swirly postmark had seemed
as close as we'd ever be again. But *Z-Cars*, Wimpys,
Jaffa cakes, Sunbeam Rapiers and 100 other dodgy
TV shows and unreliable brand names – tragically
unknown in rural Australia – sprang back to life now,
while the treat of another long-haul flight, that weird
hoovering sound inside the plane and the nothingness
of floating in the dark for almost a day, just added
to the magic. The sensory extravaganza to come had
me wriggling impatiently through an early autumn at
school, as did the pretty amazing news that we'd be
arriving in London on 5 May, the very day of the FA
Cup final.

I'd just about split at the seams by the time the 747
lurched free of its moorings at Melbourne airport and
it felt like weeks before we touched down in England: I
was fairly certain I never wanted to hear that hoovering
sound again. We traipsed along Heathrow's millipede
trail of walkways, Mum and Dad washed out, Anne
bemused, and John and I grinning like idiots. We were
still smiling an hour later in a lunchtime traffic jam in
transit to my grandparents' semi-detached home, the
congestion caused partly by Leeds and Sunderland fans
heading beyond us to Wembley. Studying the flow of
intense faces, red-and-white scarves and Triumphs,
Zephyrs and Anglias creaking past at walking pace, we
only gradually realised we were in danger of missing

the kick-off on TV. A little too close to 3 p.m., we squeezed past a monolithic hedge and into the gravelly driveway in Park Avenue, Enfield.

'Dad grew up in this actual house' was one of a number of reflections that might have occurred to me, but didn't, as we knocked on the heavy, wooden front door. A battalion of aunts, uncles and cousins had gathered to greet us and to watch the game, not necessarily in that order, and we were ushered amid hugs and handshakes – largely taking place a foot or two above me – into the sitting room (*That's what everyone calls a lounge room here*, I recalled with a soothing familiarity), in time to watch the players warming up under the same grey sky as us.

As someone who hardly knew a goal net from a hair net, I was grateful that almost every cousin and uncle I'd ever heard of was there and could help fill us in. First up, it was clear Sunderland were the sitting-room favourites, partly due to their being a second-division side and thus odds-on to get hammered; also, because their opponents were Leeds United. Leeds wore angelic white but they symbolised, according to purists and uncles of the day, all that was wrong with modern football, wringing the romance out of the sport with their cynical ways. Eamon Dunphy, an Irish international player, compared their niggling tactics – allegedly a ninety-minute regime of harassing the opposition, always staying *just* on the right side of the referee – with having someone run up to your desk all day at work and stick a pin in you. The cumulative effect, he claimed believably, was demoralising.

The first soccer game John and I ever watched in full would turn out to be one of the great Cup finals. Sunderland held their own against the Leeds bullies and amazed even themselves by taking the lead after half an hour. Leeds retaliated and in the second half, with shots raining in on him like hailstones, the Sunderland goalkeeper Jim Montgomery made a phenomenal point-blank save, then corkscrewed around to deflect a second shot onto the crossbar. It was so unbelievable the commentator shouted '1–1!' and it was a second or two before we realised the ball hadn't gone in.

Twenty-five minutes later Sunderland had won the 1973 FA Cup final 1–0, sending the Park Avenue sitting room – the Australian wing, anyway – into a maelstrom of quiet stupefaction. We sat, mouths agape, as the Sunderland manager Bob Stokoe madly sprinted across the ground in his shabby raincoat and trilby to hug Montgomery, while the rest of his red-and-white-striped team mates piled deliriously on top of each other. The commentator was saying again and again, '*One of the biggest FA Cup shocks ever*'.

I was hooked, and inside twenty-four hours had bought every soccer magazine within my 10p-weekly budget, almost burning holes in them page by page in memorising the contents. John read them too, just a little less manically. And had we needed a personal brush with the glamour of the game to crystallise our nascent obsession, it was potentially less than 150 yards away. Grandad, not displeased that his now-Australian-accented grandsons had latched onto this very British preoccupation, mentioned that Alan Gilzean, Spurs' Scottish international striker, lived just up Park Avenue. He was prematurely balding, Grandad added helpfully. John and I quickly confirmed the story, finding a photo of Mr Gilzean in *Shoot!* magazine, and we spent the next few weeks stalking his house in vain for a glimpse. One day from the upstairs window I thought I spotted him in a car as it hurtled past, but John, who read science magazines, was sceptical.

The cosy, beige-tiled kitchen at Park Avenue owed its distinctive aroma to Uncle Shawn's roll-your-owns. John and I sat there that summer, listening to Dad, Uncle Kevin, Grandad and himself mulling over soccer stars from a couple of decades before. Soaking in the ambience, and occasionally inhaling it, coughing quietly and contentedly, we learned of a string of folk heroes named Albert and Stan; sometimes Dixie or Patsy. It didn't matter if they had girls' names – we were entranced by the glorious, embalmed history of it all.

While football wisdom seeped from every corner of the house, Uncle Shawn stood out even in that company. A veteran of hundreds of Arsenal matches, he'd been completely deaf since he was sixteen after nearly losing his life to meningitis. He was easy enough to understand, though, and John and I watched, fascinated, as Uncle Shawn, Dad and the others careered through the reams of sign language required to hold a frenetic conversation. We picked it up ourselves as well, and were soon spelling out questions like, 'Were you joking when you said that Ted Drake scored seven goals for Arsenal against Aston Villa in 1935?' Which, admittedly, took ages.

'Tie a Yellow Ribbon Round the Old Oak Tree' was number one on the charts and British Prime Minister Ted Heath was struggling to deal with the impending oil crisis as the price of petrol spiralled beyond a pound a gallon. Of more pressing importance to me, however, was being able to watch soccer games on television every second day – like Christmas morning three times a week. England played Scotland; Northern Ireland played Wales; Juventus played Ajax in the European Cup final. In the build-up to each game I'd read *Shoot!* inside out, with Grandad and his research team providing supplementary match previews, and in any gaps Uncle Shawn would reel off extra names and facts from uneventful, long-forgotten 1–1 draws with Huddersfield Town at the rate of a pocket calculator.

After a few years in the civic-minded tidy towns of Victoria, Dad couldn't believe how dirty London was, but I hadn't noticed, blinded by the shimmering monuments of suburban Enfield. For between football matches, and just the far side of Mr Gilzean's home, was another slice of Fantasia: Cecil House. Enveloped in asphalt, it was the dullest of multi-storey buildings, but it happened to be the worldwide base for the *Guinness Book of Records*. Uncle Den took me and John there, and it was only slightly less like Willy Wonka's Chocolate Factory than I'd hoped. I'd pictured a world-record-sized theme-park kind of place, but this was more like a doctor's waiting room. There was no world's tallest person – Robert Wadlow, 8 feet 11 inches (possibly deceased) – strolling around, no sign of the dark-skinned wiry man with the 20-foot-long fingernails. The expedition was verging on anticlimactic: then we met Norris McWhirter.

Norris and his twin brother Ross were the founders of the Guinness book – John and I knew it was either his or his identical sibling's photo on the inside cover of the books – and it was brilliant to see him just strolling around this nondescript office. A kindly middle-aged man with a Celtic lilt, he listened as we told him we knew the Burkes of Horsham who held the Australian record for the heaviest-ever triplets at birth. We said they lived in the same street as us (which was true) and he seemed quite excited by the news. I think.

Between alleged sightings of balding soccer stars and actual encounters with Guinness twins, England's mystical status was sealed, and a three-week trip to

Ireland was like being dragged out of the toy shop.
We drove to Liverpool and caught the ferry overnight
to Dublin, where cars were rustier and *Shoot!* arrived
a critical day or two later. From there it was an ocean
of Irish culture – farms, nuns, country lanes that went
for months – with relatives sharing amusing tales with
Mum and Dad way over my head.

Mum's two brothers, Uncle Diarmuid and Uncle
John, were both priests – it was a family speciality – but,
like Uncle Den, entertaining despite the impediment.
They provided the highlight, buying us our first-ever
soccer ball at a County Kerry service station; apparently
flouting their vow of poverty with a £2 splurge. But
despite having a brilliant time with them hacking the
ball in a heavenly direction on a craggy, wind-torn
beach, we instinctively knew there was even more fun
to be had a tantalising 50 or 60 miles back across the
Irish Sea.

Finally we returned to London, where I spent our
last few days trying to suck the Englishness out of the
air and make it stick. Saying goodbye to everyone was
easier for my parents this time, but harder for me. I
could get used to living in a country where uncles talked
football and police booths looked like Tardises. As we
prepared for another twenty-four hours in space, all I
felt was longing for the home I was about to leave a
second time.

The Zoot Suit

To the best of my knowledge, I'd never met anyone from a Wimmera state school. I wasn't sure what went on at places like Horsham Central, the school that bordered ours, and I couldn't help but be suspicious of their ill-fated Protestant universe. I'd only heard rumours about a weird, watered-down God, but where was the clarity, the conviction, the first Communion? Deep down, it had to be chaos.

Theologically, transubstantiation of the Eucharist and the infallibility of the Pope may have been the overriding concerns, but locally the abuse from over the fence was more pressing. The triumphal Protestant chant, 'Catholic dogs, Stink like hogs,' rang out from next door every now and again and it stung like sunburn. It was witty (by then-current standards), concise and it rhymed perfectly. We'd shriek back similar but clumsier jibes and, frankly, without a poet or songwriter in our ranks, we knew we were well beaten.

These heresy-stained lunchtimes weren't the only distraction on the road to Australian adulthood;

there was also the unmistakeable tinge of Irishness permeating the playground. Apart from the occasional Irish accent of a priest or nun, and the undulating field of deep green jumpers, skivvies and skirts during assembly that might have reminded near-sighted onlookers of Connemara, there was also St Michael's & St John's Primary School 'house' system, which divided us into four groups for school sports: Tara, Clontarf, Kildare and Melleray. On athletics day in the dead heat of summer, as my body puckered like a slowly shrivelling lemon during the 400 metres, native trees providing scant shelter as I stumbled to a third-last-place finish, there was the minor consolation of having done my house, Tara, proud: Tara being a village in County Meath near Dublin, on the verge of a hill that was the historic seat of ancient Irish kings.

This array of Brigidine nuns and Gaelic monarchs was, in its own way, as cosy as a warm lap, and it didn't seem promising that when my family moved across town to Federation Avenue, the boy next door had a dubiously agnostic look about him. Robert Lowe was blessed with more swagger than you usually found just off Natimuk Road, and with his height and frame he was intimidating. He was a nice bloke, though, and – call this faint praise, if you like – one of the most comically gifted ten-year-olds I'd ever met.

If John and I had been fused at the hip, four arms flapping ready for battle, Robert could still have had us for breakfast. Fortunately we had enough in the way of mutual interests, such as dragsters – the ones with pedals – and TV, to establish a friendship, and we set the alliance in stone by sometimes scuffing a soccer ball about in his front yard, avoiding his mum's anxiously crafted flower and shrub arrangements, and ours. The Papal issue hadn't come up.

We'd been back in Australia for a year. It was a struggle settling in at first, and the stockyards, farm-machinery retailers and Firebrace Street's catwalk of dust-caked utes had never looked less appealing. Within weeks, though, England resumed its revered but distant role, as the less dreamlike world of schoolwork, drying the dishes and altar-boy training took root again. Nevertheless, we'd picked up one durable souvenir from our travels, the epicentre of which was the shrine in our bedroom, and in a spirit of neighbourly goodwill Robert was deemed worthy of a visit.

He was impressed, or at least not visibly horrified. Perhaps my brother and I lacked something in the subtleties of interior design, but we were passionate to a fault. External glass aside, and allowing some breathing space for the crucifix on the dressing table, nearly every available square inch in our bedroom was swallowed by soccer paraphernalia. The posters behind our bedheads and surrounding walls featured the entire first division, with double-page team portraits of everyone from championship contenders Leeds, Derby County and

Burnley to lowly Norwich City and Manchester United (sadly struggling against relegation), a riot of reds, yellows, blacks, and half-a-dozen shades of blue. A couple of hundred pale British and Irish faces stared out at us with fixed pre-season smiles; oddly, I seldom had nightmares.

Arsenal, being just one of twenty-two teams in the top flight, only figured in *Shoot!* every three or four issues, and with cupboard doors dedicated to the club we were forced to cobble together whatever Gunners detritus we could to add to the mosaic; even a slab of text about Arsenal looked good to us. Alex Cropley, a new signing from Scottish club Hibernian, was determined to make the grade at Highbury and said as much in 500 words or so. With the interview pasted next to my bed, I could have quoted him more confidently than Psalm 23: and I'd sung 'The Lord's My Shepherd' every Sunday for months.

The start of the 1974/75 soccer season brought fresh challenges for us all. For my part, there was a tricky concoction of yellowed edges of paper and curled dried-up strips of dead sticky tape in replacing the relegated Southampton, Norwich and Manchester United teams on the montage with first-division newcomers Carlisle United, Luton and Middlesbrough. With the freshly white-bordered posters bright among their more experienced rivals, the regeneration in the changing season felt almost organic.

I was in the final stages of becoming oblivious to the outside world. We'd been in Federation Avenue for a while now and it was yet to be remotely relevant to me that we were living in perhaps the only H-shaped residence in the western hemisphere. You'd enter through a deceptively normal front door only to discover the house immediately split into an east and west wing. Making your way to the rear of the place via either wing, you'd realise there were more back doors than strictly necessary; sprouting from every conceivable corner, there were four all told. Adding to the quirky scenario, each exit led to a gargantuan willow tree in the backyard that dwarfed the outer Horsham skyline.

Having a tree the size of the Eiffel Tower half a cricket pitch away from my bedroom window might have been slightly embarrassing had I given it a moment's thought. It certainly troubled my parents, who had nightmares about how much damage the roots of a killer willow tree clawing underground like a triffid might wreak on the community. A plumber's truck parked outside any house within a half-mile radius was reason enough for at least a twinge of guilt.

Meanwhile, next door, in a house more vulnerable than most to our grasping willow, Robert had been plotting. Uninspired by the meticulously tended rose bushes on his side of the fence, our renegade neighbour needed something more abstract to fulfil him. Although rebellion was inevitable, he was years ahead of his time in the vehicle he chose: a proprietary company. Mucking around in our garden after school one afternoon, with the willow tree's spindly branches, as ever, scraping in the breeze, John, on his Super Elliott bike, was stopped in his flattened grass tracks, while I spun slowly to a standstill on the Hill's Hoist.[5] We were taking in Robert's Moses-like pronouncement: 'Let's form the Zoot Company'.

As Robert outlined his prospectus, the words 'Zoot' and 'Company' began to spell pure excitement. He explained that it could be an organisation devoted to … well, it could make, um … a comic called *Zoot*, say, and … uh, heaps of other stuff. We'd need our own cartoon characters, Robert coolly reasoned, and as a template he'd drawn something called a dinglepuss, a term of abuse he'd recently heard at school. Though his master plan was still a little sketchy, clearly hours, if not years, of entertainment beckoned.

With a sheaf of unlined quarto pages stripped from one of Mum's writing pads, the three of us began to map it out over the next twenty-four hours. Effortlessly we invented enough characters to fill *Zoot* issue one: 'A racing car driver, Rod Hott,' John said; 'Gorse Horse, or how about, um, Mog the Dog?' Robert offered intently; 'Martin Shivers,' I suggested – a cartoon ghost, *a la* Casper, whose name was an improbably cunning play on the Tottenham centre-forward, Martin Chivers. It was too easy.

That Wednesday, *Zoot* hit the streets – Federation Avenue, anyway. We admired our handiwork, flicking through it a couple of times – not bothering to show it to anyone else, like our other friends for instance – before immediately embarking on issue two. We burrowed into the routine, with Tuesday evening an arbitrarily imposed weekly deadline, but sacrosanct nonetheless; sneaking from our beds after lights-out to finish a few pages quickly became the fashion.

We settled into our new lives as comic geniuses, cottoning on to a cartoon formula of a few frames of frenzied – unintelligible, if necessary – activity between a string of characters with one of them delivering a cringingly bad pun to round things up. There was a cast of talking dogs, cats, poultry, wishing wells, and others, maybe appropriated from *Sesame Street*, *Lost in Space*, *Butch Cassidy and the Sundance Kid* – whatever grabbed us. We were bored easily, though, and discarded characters almost as soon as we'd created them. The casualty list was extensive: among dozens rapidly consigned to the history books were Superchook, the sorry inhabitants of Floptown ('Every cartoon they're in could be their last,' we declared prophetically) and the fiendishly evil Lucky Ducky.

However, one deadline a week wasn't enough and the Zoot franchise inevitably spread its wings. With John's and my love of cars still idling in the background, we launched *AutoZoot*, featuring lopsided drawings and scratchy 60-word descriptions of the latest models, as well as a possibly bogus letters page. 'Q: I have a 1964 Holden EH Premier 179 CID 2 barrel six and how should I replace it with a 350 CID 4 barrel V8 5750cc's engine? A: I suggest you ask someone else.'

The enterprise continued to flower. Aussie-rules star Alex Jesaulenko had lent his name to a new chocolate drink called Yoo-hoo ('You too should drink Yoo-hoo' was Jezza's irresistible siren song), promptly inspiring our own 'Zoot-hoo', which, under close scrutiny, could have been exposed as little more than Milo with extravagantly doctored labels. In a similar tradition came 'Zoot-ball', about which nay-sayers complained that a perfectly respectable sport called four-square – which happened to have identical rules – was already in existence. The Zoot branding, though, gave it our elusive stamp of approval.

We were beginning to feel unstoppable, but we soon overstretched ourselves: not with the ZGA – the Zoot Golf Association – which hosted occasional minigolf tournaments at Robert's place, but rather the ill-starred Zoot Navy. The Navy's purpose was vague, what with Horsham being a couple of hundred miles inland and all, but there was still a certain logic behind John's proposal that anyone wanting to be sworn in had to have a *Herald* swimming safety certificate.

Perhaps it was inevitable the Catholic/Protestant divide would rear up at some stage and the fact that

John and I already had our *Heralds*, and Robert didn't, led to a difficult impasse. John put his foot down and the backyard six-day war was on in earnest. My brother and I weren't too worried about a skirmish – after all, it was a matter of public record that we could swim 50 metres unassisted – but Robert had seen red and enlisted the help of another state-school kid to bellow the 'Catholic dogs' slogan at regular intervals from next door.

John and I didn't descend to their level – neither of us had great voice projection – but after a stand-off lasting the first half of a school week there was a bit of a scuffle, a punch, a push and a shove and, honour satisfied, we became friends again. Given that Robert was twice our size, it seemed a fair result. The Zoot Navy, however, was dead in the water.

Former Skyhooks lead guitarist Red Symons has written that children are capable of absorbing very large amounts of information provided it has no useful purpose. As I hadn't twigged that newspapers were an excellent source of intelligence on a range of subjects, possibly including soccer, I was almost solely reliant on data gleaned from the pages of *Shoot!* to prove him right.

Shoot! arrived via sea mail, three months out of date when it was trucked into Horsham. Living a life skewed thirteen weeks behind the real world didn't faze me, though. Secure in the belief that I wasn't being scooped by any soccer fans this side of the equator, the weekly appearance of the magazine in a newsagent on the cusp of the Little Desert retained a faintly miraculous edge.

However, trumping that was the aeroplane-fast world of TV, more specifically *The Big Match*. The English soccer program, hosted by the genial Brian Moore, featured the catchiest theme music known to humankind (ask a Londoner to whistle it for you some time), and the opening titles of the show were my favourite thirty seconds of the week. Sadly, *The Big Match* only had highlights of two or three games, so you needed to get lucky to stay in touch with your team.

Thanks to Brian Moore, the broad canvas of my sporting life was only a week or so out of date, but tantalising details stayed months in arrears. I knew Liverpool was in the FA Cup final, for instance, but Arsenal could have been seventh or seventeenth and I wouldn't have known for sure, except we probably weren't seventh, i.e. any good, because *The Big Match* never showed our games.

Despite inhabiting a parallel universe three months and 12,000 miles away, I somehow discovered there was an Australian national soccer team; and not only that there was one, but that the one there was had just qualified for the first time for the World Cup finals to be held in West Germany. If anyone had asked, I could have recounted the post-match elation of Alan Warboys and Bruce Bannister after scoring hat-tricks for third-division Bristol Rovers in an 8–2 hammering of Brighton & Hove Albion, or the funny thing Liverpool's Scottish manager Bill Shankly told journalists when he signed the giant defender Ron Yeats ('Goo on … take a walk aroond him'). But because there wasn't an Australian equivalent to *Shoot!*, I knew nothing about the Aussie soccer team, other than the fact they'd recently been dubbed the 'Socceroos'.

I hadn't yet mustered much enthusiasm for Australian sports stars at large, but this was different. It was a bunch of part-timers – labourers, milkmen, private detectives – tackling the best players on Earth, and that had a certain ring to it. The name 'World Cup' seemed pretty definitive too. Anything as equivocal as a 'Test match', or dedicated to a Davis, had to suffer in comparison.

Surviving a 4 a.m. wake-up call, and with a pack of Lolly Gobble Bliss Bombs to sustain us, Dad, John and I, in a row of faded, checked dressing gowns, settled in for the first of Australia's three World Cup games: against East Germany. It proved hard to watch in most respects. On black-and-white TV, Australia's green and gold was almost indistinguishable from the blue and white (apparently) of the Germans, and, still groggy in the pre-dawn, I had no idea who was winning each 50–50 challenge as East Germany mounted a footballing blitzkrieg in the Wimmera darkness. One of the twenty light-shirted outfield players finally found the net after fifty-six minutes; perhaps appropriately, amid the confusion (mine, anyway), it was an inadvertent own-goal for the Germans by Australia's Col Curran.

The Socceroos were beaten 2–0, defended stoutly again in their next match, a 3–0 loss to the eventual champions West Germany, and I cheered blearily as Australia stole a scoreless draw against Chile. It was grim viewing for the most part – barracking for a team that was about 1000 to 1 to win the Cup wasn't meant to be easy – but although my heart was frequently in and around my mouth as the Aussie brick wall withstood a battering over 270 distended minutes, in some ways it was a remote experience.

Bear in mind that none of the Australian team had been guests on *Hey, Hey, It's Saturday!*, *The Mike Walsh Show* or even country Victoria's own *Six Tonight*. Doug Utjesenovic hadn't been spotted on BTV-6 doing ads for runners, or Peter Wilson for a high-fibre breakfast cereal, the sort of thing that makes you feel closer to a player. Utjesenovic, Wilson, Johnny Warren, Atti Abonyi and the rest of the Socceroos remained – as individuals – as much of a mystery to me at the end of the World Cup finals as they'd been at the start. And no-one else at St Michael's & St John's even seemed to notice that the tournament had taken place.

Despite their negligible impact in key areas of regional Victoria, in the bigger picture the Socceroos had left an impression. I'd felt the millions of pairs of

German and Chilean eyes on the soccer players of our irrelevant island, and while the breakfasting habits of a ragtag team mightn't have been recorded, the feats of the Socceroos had *mattered* to the rest of the world. In the same week, the other World Cup outsiders Haiti and Zaire were smacked 7–0 and 9–0 and our results looked even better. It had to make you proud, although I wasn't sure what of exactly. Proud to be … Australian? Nope, that didn't sound right.

With our sectarian problems behind us the Zoot Company was primed for expansion again, and John and I knew where to head for inspiration: *Tiger and Scorcher*. As with most items associated with England – flip-flops, anoraks, plimsolls and the like – the eccentric name of this real-life comic (the unsettling result of a merger between *Tiger* and *Scorcher* magazines) caused me endless embarrassment: in this case, whenever I warily requested it at the newsagent to the smirking disbelief of the teenage girl behind the counter. But one *Tiger and Scorcher* character, the brilliant Roy Race, aka 'Roy Of The Rovers', salved the wounds.

In Roy's weekly adventures with fictional Melchester Rovers, he'd battle a niggling calf, an ancient gypsy curse or a strangely unhelpful referee in clashes with surly, possibly corrupt Russian teams in the European Cup Winners' Cup and, from a couple of goals down, he'd invariably bring home the bacon.

Naturally I was hooked, and in that fine line between *homage* and blatant plagiarism I established my own soccer character – Ron Dodgers. Ron played for fictional Skemford City and his name was a cunning play on the former Swindon Town and Queen's Park Rangers forward, Don Rogers. To muddy the plot, my imaginary hero also had a brother, Terry, and soon Ron and Terry Dodgers found themselves with dicky calves, curses and uncompromising Russian opponents of their own.

Perhaps with a lime cordial or two too many under my belt, I later engineered a transfer for the Dodgers brothers to the very real Ayr United, a workmanlike team from the lower reaches of the Scottish first division (nickname – The Honest Men; club address – Somerset Park, Tryfield Place, Ayr KA8 9NB, Scotland. Why not drop them a line?). Then, in a team overloaded – to the point of statistical improbability – with players named Jock, the Dodgers transformed my fictional Ayr United into a European superpower. Ayr United 4, Barcelona 3 was a typically preposterous score line in an early European Cup fixture.

I'm not sure what Robert made of this unusual turn of events, the world game's infiltration of *Zoot* ranks, but I think he understood that his was a localised case of having to assimilate with the immigrants. In any case, Robert – an Aussie-rules and cricket fan by breeding – had been happy enough to become a key player in our marathon backyard soccer matches, dummying around bushes and clothes lines and belting shots at John or at the once-white garage wall. Fictional British footballers nestling alongside Superchook and Lucky Ducky probably seemed part of the same bargain.

In a similar spirit Robert opted to barrack for Queen's Park Rangers, whose blue-and-white hoops mirrored those of his VFL side, Geelong. But although Rangers were in the midst of the most successful period in the club's 90-year history – they had an infinitely better team than Arsenal – his interest in QPR threatened to be usurped by humble Workington FC.

A club from the lead-skied, coal-stained, crumbling, choking north of England as we imagined it, Workington propped up the fourth division like they'd signed an annual agreement, winning as few as four games out of forty-six in their worst of several consecutive disastrous seasons. To us budding football romantics and would-be satirists, their plight was irresistible.

We knew their players only by name (they'd never make it as far as British television, never mind rural Australia), but to us they became vivid, almost surreally cartoonish characters. The likes of Tony Geidmintis, Ronnie Walker and shell-shocked goalkeeper Mike Rogan were real enough professional footballers trying to make a living in an unlovely (we'd decided) part of

England, but poetic licence was patently there for the taking.

With the success among our audience of three of the drizzly Highland adventures of Ron and Terry Dodgers, a specialist soccer publication seemed well within our mandate, and as a tribute to the fourth-division club we began to produce our own Workington match programs. Occasionally written on tissue paper, for extra cash-strapped effect, we'd include highlights of the previous week's match, with drawings of, say, the Workington team doing a lap of honour after winning a corner-kick. Most pictures were self-explanatory, although captions like 'Own-goal scorer gets a kindly punch in the head from team mate Walker' added to the local colour. And our match previews were incisive: before a fictitious FA Cup tie between Workington and Liverpool, we predicted the Liverpudlians would adopt a defensive approach, with goalkeeper Ray Clemence 'under strict orders not to stray into Workington's penalty area'.

Robert was getting into his stride, conjuring up a bogus, somewhat unimpressive major sponsor for the club – Mario's Fish & Chip Shop – as well as a new coach, the hopelessly cheerful Hughfus McGurk, whose 'I'm forecasting an enormous crowd' catchcry went unheeded for years at a time. Robert also decided our match programs needed input from the Workington supporters' club, its president a cartoon pig called Andrew Smedley. His drawings of Andrew with a massive red-and-white woolly scarf trailing around his tail had me and John in stitches, although the post-match barbecues Smedley flamboyantly advertised on his regular social page might, from a pig's-eye view, have been considered in questionable taste.

Amid the general air of desperate optimism, only the unnamed editor of the magazine could inject a rational tone. One week, Timbuktoo FC happened to be in town 'visiting Workington to see a coalmine', and a fixture was hastily arranged. With the African visitors featuring such unlikely players as Hfkcn, Wehskxmv, Tyeksbxmx and Dog, our editor observed, 'It promises to be a great match as both sides will be out to draw or lose by a slight margin.'

It was a rare moment of cool analysis, despite the difficult logical territory of two teams hell-bent on drawing or losing with dignity. Absurdity sat pretty well with us, though, given what was filling our heads while the outside world raged over Watergate, the Khemlani[6] loans affair and Sherbet v Skyhooks.[7] In our two-house universe of *AutoZoot*, Terry Dodgers, aborted naval exercises and football coaches called Hughfus, reality and reason were in short supply.

Part II

Part II

Track Down

Sitting at my computer in the Melbourne Cricket Ground media area, the parachute-baggy Socceroos shirt still hung slightly heavy on me. While I was almost monomaniacally focused on the Australia v Iran match being played out only metres away, there was still a synapse or ganglion or two, pulsing in my brain in the background, mulling over my choice of attire. Would a morning suit have made a better impression? Perhaps a cape? Given my domestic circumstances at the time, though, upward mobility might have been a bit of a lost cause.

The bottom line was that I lived in a shed. Or maybe it was a tram. Actually, a friend's mum had taken a walk around my granny flat out the back of a run-down five-bedroom house in inner-urban Melbourne, and come to the conclusion it was a converted railway carriage. The outer walls of the place – reconstituted plasterboard with just a hint of asbestos – disguised it sufficiently that no-one knew quite what it was. It was the first place I'd ever lived in alone, though, and I was pretty much convinced it was an unbelievably cool *pad*.

To be honest, I was living sort of a primitive existence. The shower was situated just outside the front door, the toilet was fully 20 metres away at the other end of the block, and the wiring was sufficiently precarious that whenever you used the hot water you could feel an electric tingle in your fingers. It reminded me of our first house in Australia and you'd almost say I'd come full circle, if our old Mallee home hadn't been a few rungs upmarket. Not that I cared, for my bungalow life was effortlessly, unarguably, unenviably bohemian.

A couple of years earlier, I'd been steeped in asbestos and in between jobs when a friend of mine, Sam Prenesti, mentioned a funny thing. Kicking a ball around Brunswick Street Oval one grey September afternoon, with Sam impressed, I imagined, to be sharing the pitch with someone wearing authentic 1995/96 season Arsenal socks (away kit), he divulged – just out of interest – that he'd recently been appointed editor of a nationally distributed soccer magazine. Sam, who'd inherited the relentless Mediterranean work ethic of his parents, always had three or four careers on the go. In recent times he'd been employed as everything from house painter to independent federal MP Phil Cleary's media adviser, so his neglecting to mention the soccer job within sixty seconds of his appointment was – just – forgivable.

Soccer Australia was an unusual magazine. Published by the enigmatic Ettore Flacco, a flamboyant Italian-Australian (who'd later fulfil his destiny as the brains behind the Aussie women's soccer-team nude calendar), the most impressive aspect of it was the advertising. It carried full-page ads from Coca-Cola, Hugo Boss, Optus and others, a good effort for a small-time publication: Ettore clearly had an aptitude for wooing multinational companies. The editorial content, though, was ... variable in quality.

Occasionally, stories seemed to have been lifted from foreign-language publications and translated directly and erratically into English. Sam gave me a copy of that month's issue featuring an interview with then-Yugoslav star Dejan Savicevic, which began: 'Both the burden and joy of AC Milan supporters, Savicevic expresses the most appreciated interpretation of soccer: genius and insanity'. I was intrigued. 'It is not that he fears ruffling his chestnut-coloured curls that precludes him from using his head in playing', it continued, and when Dejan was asked the curly question about his heading failures, he confessed, 'It is difficult to perfect the aerial duels.' Granted it was almost poetic, but over the course of a few pages your head, unlike Dejan's apparently, would ache.

There was also the odd feature you'd read the whole way through and think to yourself at the end, 'Hey, that article didn't even mention soccer': you'd find it had been about women's sportswear. Then there were the cover photos of bare-chested national soccer league players with attractive women clinging to them for dear life. Ettore's three main interests appeared to be football, fashion, and people without clothes. And he was happy to squeeze all three into *Soccer Australia* magazine.

Sam's theory, however, was that there should be a whole lot of soccer stuff in *Soccer Australia*. Ettore didn't have any vehement objection to football content and didn't mind me getting involved. I started with a bit of spell-checking of Hungarian clubs and Montenegrin players, then graduated to rewriting some of the foreign-language features and, within three months, writing articles of my own. I was only doing the pieces no-one else could be bothered with – like in-depth analysis of rounds twelve to fifteen of the national soccer league – but it seemed miraculous that I could get published in a very real soccer magazine, as well as getting paid (barely) for doing it.

I was content behind the scenes, working from home in the carriage, looking for typos and penning near-anonymous articles about the NSL. It was comfortably low-risk and I figured I could probably spend the next thirty years or so in the role. Unfortunately, for some reason Sam saw me as a potential actual journalist. I wasn't so sure. I suspected that a dash of shyness, a hint of cowardice and a level of diplomacy such that

I rarely committed myself even to sitting on the fence didn't point me irresistibly towards the career. Sam was insistent, though, and despite my reservations, I eventually agreed. In the end, maybe I figured that anything my brother could do, I could probably do at least half as well.

John had been a journalist at *The Age* for nearly a decade. Softly spoken but hard-nosed in his own way, he was a useful role model and, while I was aware that following in your big brother's footsteps was slightly lame, being a soccer journalist – being really *connected* to the game in a way I'd never imagined possible, and getting paid (barely) for it – was an infinitely better option than the chain of public-service jobs I'd held down in my twenties. I prepared for my debut assignment.

Here, it threatened to turn ugly. My initial task could have been to interview a timid youth player with North Geelong or a jovially overweight veteran from Melbourne Knights or Newcastle Breakers, a gentle easing in to the post. Instead, it was Paul Wade. Captain Socceroo. The face of Aussie soccer. Eighteen months earlier he'd marked Diego Maradona in a World Cup match in Buenos Aires, and since then he'd been in an advertisement for Greenpeace and appeared on the 'Battle of the Codes' edition of *Sale of the Century*. Paul Wade was big.

I dialled his number halfway through a couple of

times before abandoning the call and regrouping. He's just a bloke, I kept telling myself – but I knew I was wrong. He'd marked Maradona: he was *Wadey*. A few minutes later I summoned the courage to try again, dialling in full and hoping it wasn't as obvious to him as it was to me that I was sitting on a mattress on the floor of a railway carriage.

'Hellooww,' a voice boomed merrily like it was expecting fantastic news. I knew this was going to be a let-down for the poor guy. Surprisingly, though, even after he'd established I was no-one he'd ever heard of, Wadey still seemed delighted to hear from me. I asked the first question from a piece of paper resting on my worn bedroom sideboard and the Socceroo captain bounded in with an enthusiastic reply. In the space of ten seconds, I realised I could do this. My hands stopped shaking. A fretful career in journalism was underway.

Kidd's Alright

Mingling with the familiar aromas of cut grass and smoke from the burning-off out towards Natimuk, the distinctive deathly odour of the Arsenal Football Club had wafted as far as rural Australia. A record five championships in the 1930s, and the League and FA Cup double as recently as 1971, might have meant that Dad, Uncle Shawn and countless other Gunners fans had a safe store of pleasant memories for their old age, but where did it get us now? Two wins in thirteen games and the laughing stock of English soccer, as far as I could tell.

With the relegation of Manchester United, it was Everton, Tottenham and Arsenal claiming the longest unbroken stretches in the first division. Everton and Spurs hadn't been in division two since the 1950s – a decent run – but the Gunners hadn't been out of the top flight since 1919. And if, as seemed a fair bet, Arsenal were relegated for the first time in six decades, it had to reflect poorly on me.

Three years earlier, Charlie George had scored

the winning goal for the Gunners in the FA Cup final. It was enough to inspire a mysterious ensemble, The Strikers and Children of Selston Bagthorpe Primary School Choir, to record the song 'I Wish I Could Play Like Charlie George', which was even better than it sounds. But Charlie had fallen out with the Arsenal management and seemed to be heading for the door: The Strikers and Children of Selston Bagthorpe Primary School Choir would never record again.

A few players from the 1971 'double'-winning team had already left, including our elderly captain Frank McLintock, who'd been off-loaded to Robert's Geelong lookalikes at QPR. McLintock suddenly seemed ten years younger in the blue-and-white hoops, while I was ageing at a similar rate. I flailed around the sports pages of *The Age* in the first months of the 1974/75 season, searching in vain for a string of Gunners victories (one in a row would have been good) as the club embarked on its worst run in half a century. The fact that there were still some phantom names from 1971 parading in Arsenal colours each week was like knowing that someone in the next street had won Tattslotto a few years back.

We lost 2–0 to Leeds at the start of October and were bottom of the division for the first time in plenty of Arsenal fans' lives. Another defeat at Tottenham a fortnight later was even worse, captured in miserable detail on *The Big Match*. The only upbeat moment for the more un-Christian Arsenal fans was Spurs midfielder Steve Perryman copping a badly blackened eye, but it reminded me too much of a documentary I'd seen at school about a disfigured boy in South America called Alfredo. Blinded, bruised and battered, the Tottenham player could hardly have felt more grievously harmed than I did.

The floodlights were turned on earlier each week and the descent into an English winter came with an air of foreboding as my team dug itself into an ever-deepening trench. It might go without saying that I hadn't developed much of an internal life, but still, as the ceremonial cranking up of air conditioners and sprinklers marked country Victoria's first 30°C days of the season, I was trying to be philosophical.

Arsenal may have been crumbling, but at least I was feeling more like a legitimate fan – a tentative process, given the 50-year head start I'd conceded to others in the family. In the first week of the Australian summer, Carlisle United, who I'd been assured were even worse than we were, nonetheless beat us 2–1, but with Alex Cropley making his Gunners debut after joining from Scottish club Hibernian, I'd now been involved with Arsenal for longer than three-elevenths of the team. I was, I calculated, already more of a club stalwart than no less than 27 per cent of the starting XI. Slowly, I was making inroads.

I felt more of an affinity towards new signings like

Cropley and, particularly, Terry Mancini than to the old guard; as relative newcomers we were acclimatising to Arsenal together. Mancini, a recent transfer from our old mates QPR for just £20,000 – a pittance even in the mid-1970s – was thirty-one years old and his skills were rudimentary, but he had a brilliant sense of the absurd about him. He was all but bald, in an era when youngish men paid to avoid a hairless head, not to acquire one. Also, despite his surname he was a cockney, and despite being a cockney he played for the Republic of Ireland, courtesy of an obscure Irish ancestor.

I'd read that when he made his international debut against Poland, he turned to a team mate during the national anthems and muttered something like, 'This Polish song's a bit of a shocker, isn't it?' Mancini was surprised to learn that it was, in fact, Ireland's national anthem being played. To add to his air of eccentricity, just before joining Arsenal he'd been disciplined by the Football Association for 'taking his shorts off as he was leaving the pitch'. Regrettably, *Shoot!* didn't go into any detail about *that* story.

The crowning glory for Mancini in my eyes, though, was his teaming up with Manchester City's Rodney Marsh and a youthful Terry Venables in a guest spot on *The Big Match* Christmas program. The three of them stole the show, suggesting, in a moment of genius as far as John and I were concerned, that Middlesbrough manager Jack Charlton's jug ears made him look just like the FA Cup. Their other jokes were just as funny. And original.

Mancini would have towered over the rest of the Arsenal squad as my favourite had it not been for Brian Kidd. Another Highbury newcomer, Kidd had arrived at the start of the season from Manchester United, his claim to fame that as a teenager he'd scored for United in the legendary 1968 European Cup final. This dog-eared fact was of little consequence to me, and even the likelihood that he sported the biggest perm-cum-afro this side of *Soul Train* failed to register.

A bald defender with a witty turn of phrase was a beautiful thing, but when, in one of his first games, Brian scored both Arsenal's goals in a 2–2 draw against Luton Town on *The Big Match*, I was sold. Suffice to say, the *Shoot!* interview with Kidd, under the headline 'No Kidding – Brian's A Winner!', took pride of place in the Arsenal section of the bedroom gallery.

Kidd had ten goals to his name before the season was half over, almost as many as any Arsenal striker in the whole of the previous year. This was just one of hundreds of facts I had no-one to share with but John – as an eye surgeon I think Dad had enough on his plate – but statistics were spreading inside me like bacteria. I'd sit in the shelter shed at school counting how many minutes of play it had been since Brian had scored, maybe calculating the London League ladder – who was on top in matches between all the

London clubs that season – or ruminating upon our propping up the division despite not conceding a goal in the first half of fourteen of our seventeen matches (what ramifications did that have for the fitness of our squad?). I couldn't have been more in a trance if you'd clocked me fair on the head.

In the playground eddy of cricket, hopscotch, chasey, Aussie Rules and general mucking around and bullying, my inert preoccupation with the English winter passed unnoticed; fortuitously I'd taken out insurance. The delicate politics of the Horsham schoolyard decreed that you'd want to barrack for a footy team to avoid being called a poof (or at least lessen your chances), and regardless of the fact that I was only one of 400 or so kids at St Michael's & St John's who had no idea what a poof might be, I gathered you were better off steering clear of the label.

I'd had a Victorian Football League club to call my own for a couple of years; not much of an intrusion, but handy to know it was around. Picking a favourite team from 200 miles away could have been taxing, but in my case all it took was a punch in the stomach. The club, after a brief false start, was North Melbourne. The stomach, fortunately, belonged to my brother.

Two years earlier Dad had needed some furniture for his surgery and was steered towards a showroom in Melbourne, owned by Ron Barassi. I didn't know much about footy, although I could almost have told you that as well as being the discount king, the Ron Barassi in question was the recently retired coach of VFL club Carlton. But, with his presence on television, radio and in magazines since we'd arrived in Australia, I did know that whatever else Ron Barassi was, he was Famous.

With retrospective apologies to Sir Robert Menzies[8] and Warracknabeal's own Nick Cave, in my eyes the Wimmera had long been a celebrity tundra. Picturing Mr Barassi himself doing casually slow laps of the warehouse floor around the filing cabinets and desks, signing autographs and the like, I wanted, immediately and desperately, to be a part of this. Brutally, the dream came to naught, with only John and Dad making the pilgrimage on the day, and the hours passed slowly in a sleepy country town as Mum, Anne and I awaited the arrival of the new chairs with roller wheels and a magazine rack or two. Envious, unaccountably anxious and excited all in one, I absent-mindedly skewed my Matchbox cars off the Hot Wheels track as the dull afternoon wore out.

Eventually they made it home, with startling news. My brother had actually *met* Ron Barassi and, unsurprisingly, was breathless in the wake of the experience. It transpired, though, that this may have stemmed, at least in part, from John having taken one in the breadbasket from the premiership-winning coach. The warehouse *mise en scène* had been as magical

as I'd imagined, with Mr Barassi's casual laps taking in
a few pleasantries with Dad and my brother after the
exchange of funds, his farewell gesture to John a jovial,
fairly lightly delivered fist in the guts.

Superficial wounds notwithstanding, he'd struck a
decent blow. Excited at (a) having met someone famous,
and (b) being deemed a worthy recipient of a sucker
punch from one of the VFL's finest, John took the
pledge to follow Carlton. Elated for my brother, albeit
with a tinge of jealousy at his quite tangible brush with
fame, I, like the shamelessly favour-currying sibling I
was, followed suit in an instant.

After the dust, and John's nether regions, had
settled, the Barassi episode meant little more than
permitting an emphatic 'The Blues!' when asked the
question everyone asked; the sport itself remained a
puzzle. But there was a twist in the tale when, after a year
out of football selling chairs and flattening children,
Barassi took over as coach of lowly North Melbourne,
a club which, fifty years after entering the league, was
yet to win a premiership. When word filtered through,
John and I realised we had to do the right thing and
follow our friend across town to the minnows. The fact
that neither of us knew the name of a single Carlton
player – Alex 'Yoo-hoo' Jesaulenko aside – made the
decision less painful than it might have been.

Barassi's former club was one of the most popular
at St Michael's & St John's and hadn't had any real need

of support from a couple of lukewarm Englishmen. North Melbourne, however, had been all but soldered to the bottom of the ladder since the 1920s and boasted precisely zero supporters in my class. It was a match made in heaven for a shyly accidental rebel like me.

Under Barassi the Kangaroos hardly knew themselves and within eighteen months reached only the second grand final in their history. They lost, but the following year there was more of the same as North edged closer to a first premiership. For an Arsenal fan, it was a pleasant diversion from the perennially relegation-troubled real world; although I didn't dare let the thought crystallise, the Gunners looked years away from recovery. It was intoxicating that, for the first time in my sporting life, I was a winner.

Listening to the grand final against Hawthorn on 3WV that year, my left ear pressed against the perspex in our lounge room, I drank it in, as a one-off watching every minute of the replay on Channel 6 in the evening as the Roos thrashed the Hawks. My reward was a quiet smugness in the playground for months to come; still, part of me (well, all of me) wished it was Terry Mancini and heavy-haired Brian Kidd, rather than North Melbourne's Barry Cable and Frank Gumbleton, parading a cup around the MCG.

28 Days

Biographer George Tremlett was blunt: 'He made no secret of his weight problem,' he wrote, 'and the fact that he had to restrict himself to a cruelly punishing diet or he would burst out of his clothes (which he sometimes did – exposing a flabby waistline and the hairiest of torsos)'. Okay, so Gary Glitter had his problems, but at least he wasn't a ten-year-old kid in rural Australia dealing with the stigma of being a fan of Gary Glitter.

I was walking a tightrope. On the one hand, with its stomping drum beats and guitars, and soccer-crowd hand claps and chanting, this was easily the most exciting music I'd ever heard. On the other, Gary's impractically garish dress sense surely had no place in the Wimmera. For better or worse, Tremlett's book, *The Gary Glitter Story*, hadn't made it to Horsham, and the singer's jauntily self-deprecating tales of wearing suits made of silver paper held together by wire, and feeling like a roast chicken when he started to sweat on stage, fell on deaf ears. Here, hairy and unnecessarily glittery pop stars were taken at face value.

This was a small town so I had to lie low in the music section at Langlands' department store as I flicked through the singles box for Glitter discs. And, once bought, they stayed at the back of the collection in case anyone visited. Any inclination to shout 'Did you miss me?!!' during social studies was suppressed.

But it wasn't all rock 'n' roll that summer. Everyone in Horsham was sunnily dreaming of a white-hot Christmas, but they also had the Ashes on their minds. Cricket, like politics, seemed to be on TV for months at a stretch without me knowing even which side was which, but when a torrent of pre-publicity revealed that the Poms were coming to Australia, I could feel something brewing. And given that I was more English than England's actual captain – Mike Denness being Scottish – my responsibilities were clear.

For fear of falling behind the classroom pack, I invested some of my parents' hard-earned cash in the ABC Ashes guide and devoured every word, becoming a speed-reading armchair expert. After an initial session with the book the number that resonated was 310, England batsman John Edrich's highest Test score (not out) against New Zealand in 1965. It seemed an exorbitant tally for one person, and, it having recently come to my attention that whole teams often accumulated fewer runs, I was suitably awed. The series was starting to take shape.

One evening on the cusp of summer, Dad

mentioned a letter he'd received from one of his friends back home, Brian Glynn. I mentally switched off, assuming the next ten minutes would be littered with references to mutual friends of my parents I'd never heard of and north London street and place names that meant nothing to me. I was right.

But in the midst of the roll call, I could have sworn I heard the word 'Edrich' and I was all ears. Brian Glynn was, apparently, bank manager to the stars – one John Edrich, anyway – which was revelation enough, but there was more. Mindful of England's impending trip down under, Mr Glynn had mentioned his friends in Horsham to his customer, who said he'd try to contact us during the tour.

Having a big brother cuffed by a celebrity of the magnitude of Ron Barassi was tremendous. The notion, though, of one of the giants of world sport (doesn't 310 not out against New Zealand count for anything?) ringing up for a chat was just science fiction. Any reservations I might have had about barracking against the country I lived in – and whose soccer team I'd gotten up early on winter mornings to bite my fingernails for at the World Cup finals six months earlier – drifted into insignificance now there was a family friend coming in for England at number four.

Regrettably, there'd never been a better time to be Australian. The Test series became a 12-week demolition job on English self-esteem, with Rod Marsh,

Max Walker, the Chappells and the rest establishing, seemingly once and for all, the ascendancy of the moustache. As well, it marked the birth of the Lillee–Thomson partnership that tore through England's batting and defined an Australian sporting generation with their – if I'm not mistaken – cold-hearted brutality.

Meanwhile, we had Dennis Amiss. Kids at primary schools all over Australia got the joke in the same breath as the newspaper headline writers, and Amiss, who in a previous life had been a world-class batsman with a Test average of 50.78 (unless the ABC guide was toying with me), wilted under Australia's open-chest onslaught, averaging 19 and finishing with three consecutive ducks. Most of our countrymen politely followed suit.

As each Test match progressed from the tenuous optimism of the first day to England's abject humiliation by its merciless end, I began – stump by loosened stump – to realise I'd been better off with Arsenal. Worse, I wondered what I could possibly say to an increasingly desperate Mr Edrich when he phoned.

Something bright, hinting at better days ahead, was surely in order. But as England skidded from one defeat to the next, words became hard to come by as I searched for the right tone to adopt to our friend who, to his credit, was averaging about 28. 'Don't worry, there's always the next match' began to sound more like a threat as visiting batsmen dropped like flies, accumulating bruises atop bruises and waiting nervously for something to snap.

Barracking for North Melbourne had got me off the hook for being a soccer fan, but, given that I'd advertised it across the breadth of Grade 5, there was nowhere to hide from my ancestry. The classroom vilification amounted to little more than the odd pitying glance and the omnipresent fear of being on the wrong end of a red gut, but by the time England was 4–0 down and maybe heading for their worst Ashes defeat in fifty years, I was grateful to be a mile or two from the schoolyard, immersed in a somewhat grim summer holiday.

Courtesy of the 1973 FA Cup final, watched in the soothing company of uncles and grandparents, and with the affable Sunderland beating the villainous Leeds United, the unhelpful idea of sport dispensing justice had taken seed. After a summer with both the England cricket team and Arsenal (who'd recently lost three games to teams starting with 'C' alone), I'd been set straight.

By March my enthusiasm for the English had waned just slightly, what with having detected their timidity under pressure, hesitation with the rising delivery outside off-stump, and a pathological inability to pick up a telephone and call the Wimmera. I guess I knew the odds had been against it since the end of the tour and the England squad's departure from

Australia, but I waited till late April and the first leafy descents of autumn before finally admitting defeat. For some reason I hadn't discounted the possibility of John Edrich calling from England to apologise for not making the call.

There was just one consolation during a dark summer. I also followed the tennis at the time, and was thrilled – fleetingly – when John Newcombe beat the unpleasant American Jimmy Connors in the Australian Open final. I preened my imaginary moustache as vigorously as the next man in celebrating our Newk in the first weeks of the new school year, only distantly troubled by the growing realisation: this identity stuff was getting complicated.

Secure in Vestments?

Ken Kesey, leader of the Merry Pranksters, a battalion of hippies whose bus had blazed an erratic trail around the USA ten years earlier, put it simply: 'I want to be an earthquake, not a seismograph'. Telling the story wasn't enough, you had to *become* the story. Had *The Electric Kool-Aid Acid Test*, the famous book about the Pranksters, been a prescribed Australian primary school text, John and I, sweating from the heat of the Federation Avenue printing presses, would doubtless have nodded sagely at the Kesey decree.

The introduction of colour TV to Australia was only a matter of days away – not to our house, but that's by the by – and the Zoot Company recognised that change was in the air. Robert, John and I had each gone solo, ceasing production of *Zoot* to write our own comics which, of course, we could then show each other almost as if we had a real audience. Robert named his magazine *Rott*, John chose *Blott*, while I, effortlessly in synch, called mine *Lott*. Quickly realising, though, that the name I'd chosen was too monochrome, far too

1974, I was given the thumbs-up by Robert and John as I rebadged it *New Lott '75*.

But John and I needed more. We were young, and our undeveloped limbs were crying out from neglect at the endless, motionless hours they'd spent knotted around our production area of chairs and desks. Physiological instinct, as well as something more cerebral, was driving us. Wordlessly, we knew what was required to trigger our own version of Kesey's Richter scale – the creation of a Horsham soccer club.

Instinct and intent have their place, but sometimes you can't go past the hand of God. As devout members of the local Catholic community, Mum and Dad were part of the 'Teams Of Our Lady', groups that met once a month, maybe having dinner and celebrating a Mass at one of their homes, to supplement the regular Sunday fare. This was not, as such, my idea of a good time, but crucially one of the families my parents got to know via these Masses and meals was the Benbows. And Mr Benbow, it transpired, was an ex-soccer player.

When Dad told us, John and I were gobsmacked: in Horsham in the mid-1970s, you'd have been as likely to run into an ex-Pope. There was a former soccer player in our midst – this took some taking in – and only later did we investigate what being an ex-soccer player might entail per se. He'd been in the Victorian junior team a few years ago, Dad said, maybe the under-18s. Then he'd had serious cartilage problems and was out of the game for two years. Which more or less ended his career, Dad thought.

During the warmer months we'd have picnics with other families in the Grampians, a mountain range roughly 30 miles from Horsham. Someone would bring a footy or a round ball along, maybe cricket stuff, and the children would muck about in the shadow of a sheer rock face and slowly warping picnic tables. Pleasant afternoons were had, with the adults gritting their teeth and bravely attempting conversation through a thick stream of barbecue smoke and plumes of dust tending easterly from where a handful of kids were raising hell.

At one of these picnics, Mr Benbow infiltrated our cloudy ranks during a hybrid soccer–Aussie Rules kickabout, and with his first touch of the ball set himself apart from anyone John or I had ever laid eyes on. The ball – my birthday present a few months earlier, ingeniously smuggled into the house wrapped in newspaper and passed off as an oversized cauliflower – came to him at no great pace, but an awkward height. He sucked the life from it as he brought it to a standstill at the sole of his right shoe, then casually kicked it back as if a miracle of science hadn't taken place. You had to say it was something to aspire to.

Between the Teams Of Our Lady and the Grampian dust storms, there was talk of forming a junior soccer team. A training session was pencilled in for Sunnyside Oval with notices posted around local schools, and in a devastating marketing coup one of the priests announced the debut of the Horsham Soccer Club at Sunday Mass.

I was excited, but a tad sceptical. Most of the enthusiasm for the project seemed to be emanating from Dad and Mr Benbow, who weren't to know what a deeply daggy image soccer had at the average Wimmera primary school. It was, effectively, the Gary Glitter of sports. A couple of isolated outbreaks in the Grampians aside, I'd never seen anyone in country Victoria kick a soccer ball – you'd see as many kids morris dancing – and, like any endeavour not wholly embraced by the majority, an interest in it left you exposed to the full range of violent primary-school possibilities.

My soccer world – courtesy of Ron and Terry Dodgers' cartoon adventures at Ayr United, the boundless, unfounded optimism of Hughfus McGurk and Andrew Smedley with down-at-heel Workington, and the weekly tribulations of Arsenal FC – seemed barely to exist beyond our front yard, but that Sunday it began to stretch its boundaries. Despite the fact that soccer had hitherto been as popular in the district as homework, eighteen kids turned up for the training session. I didn't know who they were, and I didn't know what they were doing there, but as Dad, Mr Benbow, John and I looked around Sunnyside at an admittedly uninspiring group, we were astonished by the idea that for now, maybe forever, there were almost twenty soccer players in the Wimmera.

Nonetheless, it was ugly. My brother and I and a couple of others were the only ones who'd ever seen a soccer ball in the flesh, never mind addressed one with skilful contemplation. But casting an eye over their flock during a 90-minute period in which we collectively hacked as much turf as ball on a blustery afternoon, neither Dad nor Mr Benbow betrayed any doubts as to the potential of Horsham's young soccer elite.

From the start, we were an eerily disciplined group. Whenever either coach spoke, we were quiet to a man, drinking in tactical know-how like Zoot-hoo. Perhaps it was a measure of the men at the helm, the two grown-ups proving a formidable double act. Dad commanded respect with all-knowing eyebrows and peered-through spectacles – a father figure for the team. Meanwhile, Mr Benbow, who had the official qualifications to coach any team in Australia – junior or senior – was the wavy-haired, smiling enthusiast who might strike you numb with a charismatic choice of words. As it happened, we were numbstruck within a month.

The Horsham Soccer Club (under-12s) was seven or eight sessions into its existence, and twenty or so young minds inculcated with the first principles of the world game had assembled again, in our ill-fitting collection of cling-wrap T-shirts and sleeveless footy jumpers, to hear Mr Benbow's pre-training speech. He patiently emphasised that the fourteen-man rucks that occasionally clogged up a corner of the pitch, with acres of terra nullius across the rest of Sunnyside, weren't reminiscent of the Total Football played by Holland at the previous World Cup finals, and that keeping to our designated positions wouldn't kill us. His several mantras were becoming familiar enough, but we weren't quite prepared for the conclusion. 'Do you realise,' he said firmly, 'that any one of you, if you worked hard enough, could play for Australia?' He looked me square in the eye and I could have swooned. Seconds passed as everyone digested the same piercing, ludicrous idea. I could play for Australia. He was serious.

At the end of training, there was another announcement: the Horsham Soccer Club would face Ararat in a month's time. I don't know about anyone else, but I smiled expectantly. If we were to form the bulk of the next Socceroos squad, Ararat was as good a place as any to announce ourselves.

With the benefit of a few days' meditation on the subject, however, I became a little less cocky. Ararat, it transpired, was well versed in this soccer lark. Although the town could boast just 8000 inhabitants, crucially it was 58 miles closer to Ballarat, a 60,000-strong metropolis only two hours from Melbourne, and had been inducted into their world-weary ways. It was said that Ararat not only had an under-12s soccer team, but also an under-14s, under-16s, under-18s, and a senior squad that competed in the Ballarat league. Pondering the ramifications one lunchtime as I walked past the monkey bars in my usual daze, I knew I might have to reassess: on reflection, on paper, and importantly, probably on grass, the Horsham under-12s were a short journey up the Western Highway away from a hammering.

It was Sunday, a fortnight later, and I handed the glass cruets of water and wine to the priest with as devout a face as I could muster under the circumstances. John, in identical garb but less obviously agitated, was dealing with the pressure in his own way; his mind more likely on the altar bell he'd have to ring a few minutes later during the Eucharist. I felt I should be in a state of grace, that as an integral part of the Mass in my off-white robe with a muted red cross on the hood, I might be owed something for my nervous piety. And on this day – of all days – I was looking for a sign. Nothing. Though all logic cried out against it, it was as if the Lord Himself didn't know who'd won the previous night's FA Cup quarter-final between Arsenal and West Ham.

The Gunners' horror season had assumed a surprising new dimension. We'd lost to Derby recently and had a couple of players sent off, only the second time since World War II that two members of a first-division team had been red-carded in the same match. The unthinkable, unspeakable prospect of relegation loomed as dark as ever. More improbably, Arsenal were about to win English football's other major trophy, the FA Cup. God willing.

It was less than two years since I'd been in the UK for the FA Cup final, and the idea of the Mancini-inspired Gunners gracing Wembley Stadium with the world looking on was as thrilling as it was implausible; whether or not we managed the bizarre double of getting relegated in the same season. Often, seven games was as many as it took to claim the trophy, but with four replays all-up against mighty York City, Coventry and Leicester, we'd taken that long to get to the quarter-finals. West Ham were five places above us in the League, but with home advantage we were somehow – and I loved the sound of the word – *favourites* to reach the FA Cup semi-final.

We'd reached the most hazardous part of the Mass and, critical cup-tie or not, I had to put the Gunners on hold. It was the Gospel, during which the priest delivered the reading while, trickily, you and a colleague each held a candle aloft, standing face to face at the foot of the pulpit. The key was to avoid catching the eye of the other kid, otherwise it was odds-on you'd crack up; the best option being to stare meaningfully at the flame in front of you. Unfortunately, you'd sometimes go cross-eyed which, of course, would have your opposite number buckling at the knees.

Frustrated that it was twenty-two hours until the Monday papers, with everyone from Enfield to

Bahrain, as ever, knowing the English soccer results before me, giggling like a girl wasn't really on the cards. The Gospel passed soberly, likewise the rest of the Mass, and as I took off my vestments in the sacristy to reveal my regular Sunday combination of green velour jumper and matching verdant trousers I was pleased that, with the Ararat clash a fortnight away, at least there was soccer training as a distraction.

Sadly, it transpired that states of grace counted for nothing in the godless world of the FA Cup. While I was weaving a little pre-Socceroo magic at Sunnyside Oval that afternoon, Gunners fans in north London and the Gulf had been crying into their scarves. The photo in *The Age* seemed unnecessarily large: someone I'd never heard of called Alan Taylor in an all-white kit caked muddy brown, arms aloft like Jesus, two-goal hero in an FA Cup quarter-final; inconveniently, for West Ham.

Call it coincidence, call it post-traumatic stress disorder, but the onset of chicken pox was almost instantaneous. The red lumps began to appear within minutes, and John too succumbed by sunset. The FA Cup loss, sickening though it was, was swiftly put into perspective as we faced the prospect of days in bed itchily watching a skinful of scabs emerge, forbidden to scratch lest you scarred like a gangster. It seemed too cruel a punishment, even for having the gall to picture Terry Mancini as a Wembley immortal.

John and I were battling to recover for the Ararat showdown – if tediously motionless, straitjacketed, itch-ridden hours in bed counted as battling – but elsewhere in the house there were those, like my sister Anne, otherwise preoccupied. Eight years old now, blonde and (on a good day) angelic, she was deep in preparation for her first Communion the following weekend.

As part of an extensive and detailed childhood of which I was almost completely ignorant, Anne had just been measured for her white Communion gown and head-dress and, like the rest of the female half of her class, was nearing ceremonial fever pitch. I was happy for her, but couldn't risk losing focus on my own scratchy misery.

The big match was looming as one or two scabs began to bite the dust. To John's and my massive relief, Dad, a sympathetic referee if ever we'd needed one, gave us the all-clear for Ararat late in the week. This wasn't great news for everyone. My sister's excitement at her special day was muted by the realisation that she'd be spending her Communion honeymoon in the back of our Renault 16 heading down the Western Highway, the lingering aroma of her celebratory bouquet drowned in Dencorub. But that's enough of Anne. Well, it's all I can remember.

Ararat exuded an unmistakeable air of the big-time; you could almost smell the Ballarat league from there. I'd never laid eyes on a properly marked soccer ground before, and the rigidly painted white lines, freshly billowing goal nets and fluorescent corner flags combined with a scattering of chirpy parents and indifferent passers-by to create an environment as intimidating as anything I'd imagined in my fervidly itchy nightmares.

By half-time I realised I was never going to play for Australia. Although I wasn't 100 per cent fit I'd got a few kicks, but unless elevated heels became an optional extra I was always going to struggle: I could have blamed the chicken pox for a lot of things, but not the fact that I was only four foot five. The whole team, though, had been under the pump and lucky to keep the score at 0–0 against a side which had one player, wearing number 10, who was more a potential Socceroo than the rest of us put together.

A fretful mother and a resigned but resentful sister looked on, while Dad and Mr Benbow rounded us up with hoarse words of encouragement. Mr Benbow singled out our dour defender Cowboy for a particular task – welding himself to the Ararat number 10. 'This is what you're going to tell him, Cowboy,' Mr Benbow said. '"You're my man and you're not going to get away from me for the rest of the game." Say it to me, Cowboy …'

Cowboy bowed his head. 'You're my man,' he mumbled into his feet, 'and, um, you're not gunna get away.'

'Louder, Cowboy,' Mr Benbow interrupted.

Cowboy was mortified, but slowly summoned a breath from the lower reaches of his lungs and let it rip. 'You're my man,' he bellowed, 'and you're not gunna get away from me for the rest of the game!!!' The Ararat team gathered a few yards to our left seemed as startled as we were.

We reassembled for kick-off and Cowboy approached the number 10, addressing him politely as he walked past. In retrospect, you had to feel sorry for Ararat's Georgie Best, whose only crime had been that he was too good by half. Cowboy dogged his opponent for the entire forty-five minutes, crunching the ball out of play with his cumbersome Aussie Rules boots any time it came within yards of the two of them.

Occasionally Mr Benbow would call out, 'Where is he, Cowboy? Where is he?' He needn't have worried. While the game swirled and swayed around them, with me and the rest of the team beginning to get into things, Cowboy and his opponent were close enough to do the foxtrot throughout. We somehow won 2–1, with Mr Benbow and Dad reduced to throaty whispers by the final whistle.

Six weeks earlier, as far as we knew, a competitive soccer match had never been played by a team from the Wimmera. Six weeks earlier, none of us had ever been told we might play soccer for our country (although, strictly speaking, none of us ever would). We walked off the ground, eleven boyish history-makers grinning to ourselves, and I saw Dad and his co-coach embrace. My father said something quietly that Mr Benbow translated later: 'That was bloody wonderful …' It was as close as we'd ever heard Dad come to swearing. The Teams Of Our Lady might have been a little disappointed in him.

Busted

Being born in mid-June, I'd barely made the age cut-off for Grade Prep in 1969 and the rippling effect could still be seen in the Horsham pool seven years on. I was one of only three under-12 boys at my new school, St Brigid's College, and, as the swimming sports loomed closer in first term, like a Miss World candidate I mentally rehearsed the walk to my mathematically inevitable spot on the dais, be it in first, second, or at worst – no matter what diseases or disasters struck – third place.

And I was an old hand at this business. With Mum determined that her children should be able to swim – well, don't forget we were less than 200 miles inland – John and I had endured a couple of summers of 8 a.m. sessions five or six days a week, acquiring an accursed *Herald* swimming safety certificate apiece and a level of basic competence that ensured we could complete a couple of laps of freestyle and breaststroke. Eventually.

I wasn't bad at freestyle and, despite my fear of the top-bunk height of the starting blocks, gave myself the slenderest chance of bringing home the 100-metre bacon. On the day, though, in front of the usual school crowd there by compulsory acquisition – half paying attention, half stuffing grass down each other's backs – I was undermanned and came in third.

A green ribbon – stone motherless last – wasn't anything to crow about, but I knew the worst-case scenario was a similar trophy in the breaststroke. And as we three were jettisoned into the pool again an hour later, I discovered I was the only one of us who even knew the rudiments of the stroke. The other two floundered in ever-diminishing circles a few yards from the blocks while I excavated huge watery divots on the way to a 1-minute-55-ish two-lap swim. The roar of the crowd was but slightly dulled by the rumble of semi-trailers heading for Adelaide beyond the wire fence. The blue ribbon was mine.

It was only during the official presentation before the school that I realised my supreme folly. By dint of my sluggish triumph I'd qualified for the Horsham and district finals against some of the most talented young swimmers in provincial Victoria. I was, I realised with a sickening gulp, entering the realm of Kel Duncan.

Kel Duncan – people always seemed to use the full title – was the Pele of Wimmera junior swimming. We'd trained simultaneously for a couple of years, albeit leagues apart as it were, and clearly one of us was an Olympian in the making. But Kel Duncan was only the best known of a shoal of frighteningly serious Horsham juniors, several of whom might face me in the district final of the weakest of my full repertoire of weak strokes.

It was an ugly scenario: me against the Kel Duncan brigade in front of a rural, volatile, hormonal crowd, most of them cruel Protestants who, knowing their casually vindictive ways, wouldn't be slow to remark upon the minuscule Catholic kid flailing and gasping in last by a margin of 40-odd seconds. And in 40-odd seconds a crowd could build up quite a head of steam.

The wait was over far too quickly. Inter-school sports day was sunny, placid, deceptively inviting, and I marched, armed only with togs, towards an uncertain fate. I looked around and thanked my stars that, for some reason, Kel Duncan wasn't in the row of Speedos about to take the plunge. On the downside, I pondered as I scaled the Kosciuszko peak of the blocks, there were other prospective Olympic medallists either side of me.

It took just under two minutes. I dived in, bobbing to the surface, trying to ignore the foamy slipstreams fanning out around me, watching the world pass me by as I burbled slowly towards the far end of the pool. By the time I touched the aqua-stained concrete after a hundred endless metres, the Olympians and others were already showered, dressed and on their way home. Incredibly, though, as I turned a few degrees towards the outside lane I noticed some hapless loser – sorry, gutsy competitor – with still metres to swim. Then I heard the crowd – silence. No catcalls denouncing Papal authority, no rollicking sea shanty about the slowest Catholic ever to enter Horsham waters – *nothing*.

I dragged myself onto dry land and, as my trail of footprints merged with the lake of the other competitors', the indifference of the crowd was overpowering. I towelled myself off as carefully as I could: no sudden moves. I'd finished the race hours after most of the others, but in an unprecedented display of ecumenical compassion, it seemed I was to go unpunished. I tiptoed, grateful, as quietly as possible from the venue.

It had been a nervous episode, to be sure. But secondary school seemed purpose-built for apprehension, and although I'd been on terra slightly firma earlier in the term captaining the St Brigid's juniors against Murtoa High beneath the Empire State silos, and kept my head in the aftermath of the equally unsettling Jibbidy-F piano incident, I felt I deserved a break from the psychological crash course of 1976. For better or worse, a break was in the offing.

Horsham Soccer Club had refocused. There were pig raffles, pie nights and, in the last days of the Neolithic pre-video era, the occasional screening of an international soccer match at a local theaterette. England v Wales on the biggish screen was an eccentric event, the match months old and the final result leaking around the venue not far into the second half. But we'd been starved of the real thing, with just one authentic fixture since the humbling of Ararat: a return match at Sunnyside a couple of months later. Remarkably, we'd won 3–0 and I'd hammered home one of our goals, from all of 4 yards out, to briefly revive my ailing Socceroo ambitions.

Victory against the *auld enemy*, though, was quickly shaded by the phone call that shook Wimmera soccer. It was our invitation to play in the Ballarat Cup, a knock-out competition featuring teams such as Wendouree Wanderers and Sebastopol Vikings – and with names like that, they'd have to be *real* soccer clubs. The idea of Horsham being a part of it seemed miraculous: even the name 'Ballarat Cup' had an otherworldly mystique. It might be contested at grounds boasting a six- or seven-row grandstand on one side and referees dressed in the official black, while a couple of tepid floodlights couldn't be out of the question. It took days for it to sink in: Mr Smith, with his wide-eyed soccer XI in tow, was going to Washington.

Yes I was starstruck, but the big picture didn't elude me and I feared we might be underdone for the Cup, with just one pre-tournament game scheduled against neighbouring Warracknabeal (population: a measly 3000. Ha!). Otherwise there was only training and the weekly village free-for-alls in which, as well as

Dad and Mr Benbow having a kick, any stray passers-by from Horsham and district might launch themselves into the dusty fray.

One afternoon still a few weeks from the Cup, out of the blue a couple of actual grown men turned up, maybe twenty-two or twenty-three years old. As we assessed their carriage during the warm-up – full-bodied, headlong, shoulder-first – we concluded they might be familiar with the less gentle football codes; maybe a martial art or two. If I'd been on the lookout for a warning sign, the nickname of the heftier bloke would have offered a hint – Buster.

We were deep into an uneventful match and less disciplined minds were straying towards who might be on *Countdown*[9] that evening, when myself and Buster, regrettably lining up for the opposition, found ourselves zeroing in on the same ball. As he was a foot and a half taller than me, and three or four stone to the good, I might have been advised to step aside and wish him well on his way.

The rest of the team had never doubted my bravery – they knew I didn't have any – but inexplicably I skidded into the tackle, as did, as you might imagine, Buster. I had shin pads on, how much damage could he do? I had my reply too quickly by half. The ball ran loose and the game continued as Buster regrouped his tree-trunk limbs and my soccer career ground to a halt.

Bent double, I clutched my ankle and the blood

drained from my face as a kid nearby noticed I was struggling. Hardly able to breathe, I could only indicate in distressed semaphore that perhaps my boot ought be removed before its seams split with the swelling. In the meantime, the referee – Dad – who, tough taskmaster as he was, hadn't seen fit to blow his whistle for the foul, finally brought the match to a standstill.

My ankle had swollen to FIFA-regulation football size, and as I clenched my fists desperately around a couple of tufts of buffalo grass, someone gingerly – like it was an unexploded grenade – removed my boot. I'm not sure what Dad made of seeing his son with a bulging, pulsing ankle and a face like crumpled paper, but as referee/coach and, for that matter, de facto club doctor, he coolly diagnosed Wimmera Base Hospital as my next port of call.

I was lifted tentatively into the back of a car and through the stabbing pain I could hear a couple of players deep in discussion on the touchline. Tensing and releasing, I searched for the least excruciating position on the vinyl bench seat, as one of them sprinted to the window. I was trying, and failing, to look as if I was having a leisurely lie-down, that this blinding agony was a passing inconvenience. A bit of sympathy from a team mate wouldn't go astray, though. Or at least it wouldn't have. 'Can I play in your position, Pat?' he asked chirpily.

In the end there were pros and cons. On the

upside, being the first genuine casualty in the history of the Horsham Soccer Club held a certain cachet and, after all, what could be more amusing than having your leg broken by someone called Buster? But the Ballarat Cup dream was gone, and with months of rehabilitation lying ahead, in a twelve-year-old's time frame, my career might as well have been over.

It had been a harrowing day. Still half-dazed amid the disinfectant smells and shiny white walls of the ward, trying to be brave in front of Mum and Anne when they came to visit was more than I could manage. Lying in a board-hard bed propped upright on pillows, in plaster almost up to my waist, wishing I was back at home and that today had never happened, I cried with the pain and the strangeness of it all.

Mac Factor

Supermac had bow legs. 'If Malcolm's legs were straight, he'd be the tallest man in England,' a team mate of his said in *Shoot!*. I showed the article to John and we both laughed, in a not-entirely-sure-what-bow-legs-are sort of way. To be honest, we weren't that fussed about the Malcolm Macdonald limbs: for Supermac, star striker of Newcastle United, most glamorous player in the first division and, incidentally, possessor of sideburns as thick as prickly pear, was a remote figure to the average Arsenal fan; at least until Bertie Mee resigned.

The Gunners had somehow avoided the drop into the second division by four points. We'd finished the 1974/75 season in a heady sixteenth place on the ladder out of twenty-two but, sadly, had alienated some people in the process. 'I never thought I would see the day when Arsenal players fought among themselves, pulled shirts, wasted time and so freely indulged in foul tactics,' declared one of few vanquished opponents.

The fact that the team I supported was a shambling, ill-disciplined rabble wasn't overly troubling. Hotshot

Brian Kidd's dizzyingly superlative season occupied far more of my available head space, the permed striker finishing second-top scorer in the whole first division with nineteen goals. After twelve months settling in at Arsenal, who knew how many he might tuck away in the new campaign?

Try half as many. Season 1975/76 was like a faithfully dismal re-enactment of the previous season – apart from Brian notching a bare eleven goals all-up – and as I tended to my wounds in the Wimmera Base Hospital, Arsenal were descending towards relegation again. In the midst of a couple of lonely 1–0 wins, isolated, like they'd been quarantined, in a resolute community of 2–0, 2–1, 3–1 and 3–0 defeats, we thrashed West Ham 6–1 which more or less made my decade for a week or so. But it was only a fortnight before the end of the season, when we beat fellow stragglers Wolverhampton Wanderers thanks to the bald, but witty Terry Mancini's one and only goal for the club (not long before he was transferred to fourth-division Aldershot), that our 57-year run in the top division was secured.

Bertie Mee had been the Arsenal manager since 1966. For someone who'd previously been the club physiotherapist he'd done alright: leading the Gunners to only the second League championship and FA Cup double of the twentieth century looked pretty good on a CV. But having presided over the 'Here comes relegation' era that I'd stumbled upon, an ageing Bertie had decided his time was up.

Terry Neill took over, poached acrimoniously from arch-rivals Tottenham Hotspur. But Neill, a Gunners legend having spent more than a decade of his playing career at Highbury, had arguably only been installed as Spurs manager as some kind of prank. Tottenham supporters had been sceptical about the former Arsenal captain, though as he'd steered them to a deceptively healthy ninth place before he left, they hadn't had a lot to complain about. At least, not until the after effects kicked in and they were relegated in rock-bottom position the following season, anyway.

When you're a kid, change is good, change could mean anything, and with the arrival of the new manager immoderate optimism seemed to be the order of the day. A top-half-of-the-table finish and a Gunners appearance at Wembley before I turned thirty couldn't be ruled out. But, untenably upbeat as I was – and my *joie de vivre* may have stemmed partly from having my thigh-to-toe plaster cast replaced after a month by one that began below the knee – I couldn't have predicted the next turn events would take. Or, for that matter, the turn after the next turn.

Brian Kidd had scored a hat-trick in the 6–1 West Ham aberration, replayed in loving detail on *The Big Match*, but it was almost a third of his season's tally. And while I still idolised the bubble-haired ace, up-

and-comers like the Irish trio Liam Brady, David O'Leary and Frank Stapleton were vying for his crown. Twelve months earlier, the news of 1 July 1976 would have floored me: without warning (from my Australian sources, at least), Brian Kidd was transferred to Manchester City.

It hit me hard. I guess I'd assumed that anyone who took on the mantle as my Arsenal hero would, by divine right, see out his career as a Gunners stalwart, then meld into the coaching staff for the term of his natural life before passing peacefully in his sleep aged ninety, and supporters would be singing songs in his honour in a couple of hundred years' time. That Arsenal might be just another port of call for a talented player was unthinkable.

My Neill-driven fervour was facing its first test. Brian would have to be replaced, but if the new boss followed the recent Arsenal trend, there was a fair chance we'd be investing in someone I'd never heard of from, say, an obscure Scottish club like Cowdenbeath, Stenhousemuir or Queen of the South; someone with a whiff of Alex Cropley. When word filtered up the Western Highway, I couldn't believe my ears. Surely it wouldn't be Supermac? Not *the* Supermac?

Malcolm Macdonald was part footballer, part rock star, part mystic. A man unafraid to make bold pre-match predictions – that, to be fair, were usually wrong – he was so cool there'd been a photo of him in

Shoot! with singer Brian Johnson *seven* years before AC/ DC recorded *Back in Black*. Supermac had even made it as far as *The Age*, when England had beaten Cyprus 5–0 the previous season; Malcolm, not unimpressively, nabbing all five. 'Four with his head, and one to boot' was the headline. Never having heard the phrase 'to boot' before, I was suitably baffled.

By any analysis Brian Kidd would enjoy a monumental season at Manchester City, scoring twenty-one goals in a team that finished second in the League. I was effectively oblivious, though, from the end of July when Arsenal shelled out a British record transfer fee for the great Supermac. Malcolm Macdonald of Arsenal – the idea seemed absurd. The fee was £333,333, and, typically for Supermac, even that had a certain swagger.

Before sundown there was a doctored Malcolm Macdonald poster in the Gunners gallery on our cupboard door. The jaggedly cut-out, coloured-in Arsenal shirt and shorts Blu-Tacked over his Newcastle gear were fooling no-one, but John and I couldn't wait three months to see him in the red and white. And with Supermac on board, the goalposts had shifted into another postcode entirely: we'd entered a twilight zone where 6–1 wins might happen once a month rather than once in a generation.

I'd gone too far, though, and Supermac's debut for the Gunners slapped some sense into me. Ten of the

Arsenal XI had been responsible for our seventeenth-placed finish the previous season, and even against Bristol City, just promoted and playing their first match in the top division since 1911, Macdonald barely got a kick. The serenely nicknamed 'Robins' pummelled us 1–0, with a goal scored, humiliatingly, by someone called Cheesley.

For three days, I could hardly eat. You buy the best player in the country and then get turned over by a team lost in the second and third division for sixty-five years. So where did that leave us? Amazingly, five games later the answer, after a clutch of wins and draws, was third place. Supermac had scored three times as Arsenal were transformed – by my lacklustre standards – into a pounding goal machine. West Ham 0, Arsenal 2; Arsenal 2, Stoke 0 – okay, they weren't Brazilian samba score lines but having meekly lowered my sights after the Bristol debacle, I could see a happy trend here.

It was an historic time. Not only was 1976 the beginning of the Supermac era, the high-water mark of my brief swimming career and the only instance to date of my ankle swelling bigger than my head, it was also the year my friend Iestyn got a short-wave radio. Unusually, Iestyn (it's pronounced 'Yes-din' and it's Welsh for Justin, he patiently explained to me and to everyone else he'd ever met) both swore like a brickie and was the most polite child my parents had ever met; he called Dad 'sir', for instance. His parents were the first Labor voters I'd ever met – the huge poster of Gough Whitlam[10] pasted inside their front window was all the evidence I required – and his Dad smoked so their house smelled great. More importantly, Iestyn was an Arsenal fan. Then there was his short-wave radio.

I was in the picture: short-wave equalled BBC World Service equalled soccer games from England live in Horsham. That is to say, *Soccer Games From England Live In Horsham*. This was big. Almost on cue, I realised Arsenal were playing Liverpool the weekend after next, and with the Cheesley incident behind us and the Gunners on the improve, it was clearly necessary to wheedle my way into Iestyn's house for a Saturday-night stay. John, leading a more balanced existence than his half-crazed brother, had other commitments, but after sealing the deal, Iestyn and I spent a couple of days planning the snack menu and working on a 72-hour sleep schedule that would have us in peak condition come game time.

This was Arsenal – sixteenth and seventeenth the previous two seasons, but now with Malcolm Macdonald aboard – versus the mighty Liverpool – first, second, second and first the last four years. With Supermac on our side were we within light years of the best team in England? Were Arsenal's talented youngsters Stapleton, O'Leary and Brady anywhere near up to the task? And was it Iestyn's imagination or was I totally hogging the chips? These were among the issues we pondered on the night, between shovelling bags of Colvan's in the interminable, increasingly nervous wait for the witching-hour kick-off.

The pressure was getting to me. Nine o'clock, nine thirty, ten o'clock passed as a whirlpool of artificial colours and flavours coursed through me, colliding head-on with the pre-match jitters. Despite the excitement, I was beginning to suspect that Soccer Games From England Live In Horsham mightn't be quite the thing for my delicate temperament.

Finally, and after some microscopic fine tuning with the radio dial as the British announcer's voice battled through waves of static, we were as good as there among the Highbury crowd. Iestyn sat up in bed, clearly prepared for a thoroughly enjoyable two hours or so. His colleague on the mattress on the floor, meanwhile, was in need of a little trauma counselling. Go Arsenal, go Arsenal, go Arsenal, I whispered to myself, clenching everything as the action unfolded blindly in north London. It was all too much, and when the Gunners scored early in the game, I nearly fainted.

We whooped discreetly – it was about 12.20 am – but as the euphoria of the goal began to subside, the pessimist in me claimed a killer grip. Clearly, if Arsenal lost now after being a goal to the good, it'd be infinitely worse than the run-of-the-mill abject defeats to which I'd become accustomed: the rest of the game would be agony. We might have been 1–0 up, but I knew I'd struggle to get to the final whistle.

Then it happened. As a twelve-year-old, I knew little of paranormal phenomena – the Shroud of Turin, stigmata, Bigfoot etc – but inexplicably, in a desperate instant of pure mental focus, I literally willed myself to sleep. An anaesthetist would have struggled to keep up: I have no idea how, but I managed to knock *me* out.

I woke early the next morning and lay watching the sun come through the curtains, wondering (a) how Arsenal had got on, and (b) how on earth I'd done that other thing. Iestyn eventually, lazily stirred, announcing that the game had ended 1–1 with Liverpool snatching a late equaliser. 'Pity you fell asleep,' he said merrily, 'it was really exciting.' On a benignly bright spring morning in the Wimmera, a draw against the best team in England looked a decent result. It didn't seem right to tell Iestyn how much energy I'd pumped into ensuring I missed it.

Acknowledging I'd ventured too close to the fire, I returned to obsessing from a safe distance. Within a fortnight, Arsenal had clobbered Newcastle 5–3, with Supermac scoring a hat-trick against his old club and me finding out a comfortable day and a half after the fact. He scored twice against Manchester United, two more at Tottenham, and – in just about the best form of his life – conjured another hat-trick, this time against Birmingham City. We were fourth on the ladder. It was halfway through the season and my head was spinning with the possibilities.

But after Birmingham – and from nowhere – the Arsenal squad developed two left feet apiece. Another defeat against Bristol City, 2–0 to those pesky Robins this time, might have alerted me to what was to come. Amid my ever-deepening disbelief in the draining heat of the Australian summer, the Gunners embarked on an 11-match league run without a win, with elimination from the FA Cup *to boot*.

The only consolation was being slightly distracted by one or two things brewing in the Wimmera. Negotiations had been taking place that would as near as obliterate the impact of any Arsenal downturn. By the time our season was effectively ruined with an eighth consecutive loss – 2–1 against Queen's Park Rangers – I was in a whole different world.

Part III

Empire Building

Working for *Soccer Australia* magazine inured me to the vagaries of the outside world. The fact that there was a football magazine anywhere on earth that had a place for me within its glorious orbit, never mind on its staff (part-time), still had me in a bit of a spin. I'd been planning on obsessing about soccer throughout my adult life a few hours a day regardless: this was like being paid for breathing.

Speaking of which, the $3-an-hour wages didn't faze me. Having to write up a 45-minute tape of an interview with a dour, tongue-tied midfielder from Morwell Falcons didn't knock me out of my stride. Even working largely from home and transcribing interviews in the shotgun shack as midwinter winds snuck in between the shrivelled window frames couldn't curb my enthusiasm.

But while things were good, I knew there was a glass ceiling here. No matter what cards fell my way in the entrancing world of football journalism, I realised that, even prior to my installation at *Soccer Australia*, I'd experienced all but the ultimate thrill life had to offer. It had happened a few years earlier: on one day, for one sweet moment never to be reclaimed from me, I'd nearly been an Arsenal player.

In my early twenties I travelled to the UK for the first time in almost a decade. It had felt like walking into a documentary, a re-creation of childhood set pieces – from *Shoot!* with this week's date on the cover to the Chase Road house I was born in. Still, I couldn't mistake it for somewhere I belonged: not these days. While I was a native of Southgate and had lived in the suburb till I was five, home in England had always really meant Grandma and Grandad's place in Enfield. Sadly, they'd passed away, though, so this time my cousin Eric would be my host. Eric, Uncle Shawn's son, had been an errant teenager slouched uninterested in a corner of the living room during the seminal Leeds v Sunderland FA Cup final and hadn't apparently become any more enamoured of the sport in the intervening years. Things were already a little out of whack.

Arriving at Heathrow early in an icy March, I was on a train on the Piccadilly Line almost before my toes could quake at the 5°C mid-morning chill. Although I'd never admit it was anything as sentimental as looking to anoint another English home, there was only ever one place worthy of landing in my first week. God willing, I was heading for Highbury.

It had been eight, maybe nine, years since my last

visit. I wandered around the stadium in the requisite daze, then loitered in the Arsenal shop staring shamelessly at the elderly, stately employee behind the counter – Jack Kelsey, goalkeeper, 352 games for the club between 1951 and 1962, forty-one caps for Wales: a legend. I stepped out into Avenell Road from the Clock End of the ground, now the owner of a Gunners Littlewoods Cup final 1987 scarf, and back in the main entrance for a sombre walk around the marble halls of Highbury folklore, before emerging from the wooden doors into the daylight down the stone steps, feeling like I'd participated in an ancient ceremonial rite.

Cleansed and light-headed, I was a few paces down Avenell Road again, with its wall of indistinct Edwardian terraces on one side and one of England's finest Art Deco structures on the other, when a little boy in a furry brown anorak, maybe six years old, tentatively headed my way. It was almost as if he thought he knew me, but not quite. He gazed upward as I stopped in my tracks. 'Do you play for Arsenal?' he asked politely.

The expression on his face floored me: you could go a lifetime without someone looking at you like that. Just a few yards from the stadium that had paraded the likes of Ted Drake, seven goals at Aston Villa in 1935, and Charlie George, hero of Selston Bagthorpe, it was hard to fathom that one of the two of us thought I might be an Arsenal player. Regrettably, the moment would last only as long as I could sidestep the truth, and it was terrible to have to confess that the Gunners could do better than a 9-stone, tackle-shy Victorian. A reluctant 'No' struggled out from between my lips.

'Oh,' he said, slightly surprised. We smiled at each other but I could see the light drain from his eyes. I'd been excited for us both, and as he turned to the street and trotted back to his mother, I felt I'd let him down. I needn't have worried. 'No,' I heard him chirpily announce, like he was crossing me off an *extremely* long list of strangers to whom he intended posing the unlikely question, 'he isn't one.'

That night, back in Chingford, in the house Eric shared with a couple of friends, I regaled my cousin with a mystical tale of my oneness with Arsenal. Over a late-evening coffee, with a grandfather clock gently chiming behind us on the hour, I went through the magnificent rollcall: Jack Kelsey, marble halls, the Art Deco stand, the scarf, the boy, the anorak. And at one point, during an admittedly extended monologue, Eric appeared to be very nearly paying attention.

Despite our irreconcilable differences, my cousin proved to be an impeccably genial host. Elsewhere, however, the mother country had turned hostile. I spent days trekking the employment agency trail and, while the rejections were polite, they were resolute. All I wanted was a few weeks shuffling things around a desk: not too much to ask, I didn't think, for a British subject returned to the fold. But it was as if the temp agencies didn't care about me and John Edrich. Or my Arsenal results folders – plural. Like there were no bonus points for having 'used to call thongs flip-flops' on my CV. I might as well have been from Australia.

I finally found three weeks' work with a government body that processed university applications, my job being something with paper and punch cards that I'd forget for life within days. My wages were so low I was out of pocket throughout, a key factor being that I couldn't stay at Eric's forever – cruelly, his housemates wanted their home back. A couple of Australian friends happened to be in London, so the three of us stayed in a four-in-a-room backpackers in Earls Court, run by a South African with a cough-mixture habit. Then we spent a few nights at a house in Finchley where there were fifteen of us – fourteen Australians – including seven packed rigid on the lounge-room floor. On the upside, we were only charged £5 a night. I'd crawl past a battlefield of hungover bodies in the morning as I groped towards the kitchen, feeling that things had turned out a bit differently in my homeland from what I'd expected.

So that was England. A few years later, and I hadn't had the urge to try my luck there again; I was content to stay in touch by phone from the safety of the shack. Happily, in my expanded role at *Soccer Australia* magazine, the UK had begun to figure in my day-to-day operations.

By now Sam Prenesti and I were getting a little more soccer into *Soccer Australia*. While there were still more bikinis per square inch than we would have liked, our publisher Ettore had effectively given us editorial *carte blanche*, and we were soon on the trail of killer features. Within weeks we'd interviewed the commercial television heads of sport about soccer's TV prospects; chatted with the resident comedian of the AFL's[11] *Footy Show*, Trevor Marmalade; spoken to Aboriginal activist and administrator Charlie Perkins about his remarkable career in soccer; and even collared Steve Waugh, dressing him up in Socceroo kit for a photo shoot (he seemed to enjoy it, and snaffled the gear for his troubles). Any obscure idea might come to fruition, as long as it cost less than fifty bucks.

The Trevor Marmalade story proved to be a bit of a publicity coup. I was vaguely watching TV one night a couple of weeks after the interview when *The Footy Show* came on. I looked up to see Sam Newman with a copy of *Soccer Australia* magazine in his hands. Struggling to find the right camera, he held the cover in the direction of about a million people across the country for what seemed like minutes (it was twelve seconds), before sharing the following eccentric exchange with Trevor:

SAM (pointing to the cover): Trevor Marmalade, *Soccer Australia* ... you are actually leaving [the show], are you? Does this mean we're doing auditions for a would-be comic as of now?

TREVOR (enigmatically): Come on you Reds.

SAM (continuing undaunted as he opened the magazine to show the article): And a huge spread: 'Trevor's Sporting Life' ... you are actually leaving, are you?

TREVOR (with a wry grin): I might be, but is this going anywhere?

SAM: This seems to be an article about you embracing the old home country. And you're off ...?

TREVOR (looking to the camera): You'll just have to draw your own conclusions.

SAM: So, if you want to be a comedian on the show, send in your portfolio ...

TREVOR (interjecting): And let me tell you, it certainly beats working.

One of the world game's few other mentions that year on the most popular sports show on Australian TV came a few weeks later, when Sam Newman – who was proving to be soccer's best friend in the electronic media, unwittingly or otherwise – mentioned the story of the Nottingham Forest forward Jason Lee. The

striker had been transfer-listed at his club after a series
of 'cruel jokes' by the satirical English TV show *Fantasy
Football*, in which he was taunted by the program for
his alleged 'pineapple head', as well as for missing a
succession of goal-scoring chances over the course of
a couple of months.

It was a mysterious story to be sure, and when I
heard that the co-host of the infamous show, Frank
Skinner, was coming to Melbourne for the local comedy
festival, I teed up a meeting. I arranged to take Frank to
the South Melbourne v West Adelaide national soccer
league match, after first dining royally with him at one
of the hemisphere's cheapest Chinese restaurants (it
was a very *Soccer Australia* interview).

Between mouthfuls at the restaurant and rare
moments of goal-mouth action in an unfortunately dull
match at Bob Jane Stadium, Frank explained something
of the Jason Lee scenario. Week by week that season, the
Forest striker with the distinctive bunched dreadlocks
that could, in a dark alley, be mistaken for an edible
tropical fruit, had missed the odd easy scoring chance,
which, in the great comic tradition, *Fantasy Football* had
highlighted.

This had been one of a few running gags on the
show, but when Forest put Jason on the transfer list, his
confidence shot after a run of outs, Frank, on holidays
at the time, was shocked. 'I was in San Francisco when I
got a fax from my manager which was a headline in *The*

Sun saying "Skinner and [Frank's co-host] Baddiel ruined my career." At the time I had mixed feelings, because I didn't like the idea that anyone had got really upset.'

'Is Jason's the only career you've ruined?' I asked tactfully.

'So far ...'

I bought Frank a South Melbourne scarf, and after the match he was happy to assume the obligatory pose. A few months later, when he showed the scarf on *Fantasy Football*, I almost felt I'd got my $20 worth.

Interviews with Marmalade, Skinner and others aside, the biggest coup was getting Martin Tyler on board. Tyler, a Sky-TV commentator, was to British and Australian ears pretty much the sage of soccer, and a world away from your average asbestos-ridden young local. I was developing the barest inkling of a journalistic streak and when, by chance, I got hold of Tyler's phone number, I dialled it. A voice I'd only ever heard through television speakers, enunciating phrases like '*That* is the authentic Roberto Baggio!' resonated down the telephone line from his home in Surrey. Hopeful, as ever, that I was conveying the impression of presiding over an expansive desk in an office blessed with harbour views, rather than an undulating mattress on a floor surrounded by scratched plasterboard walls, I invited Martin to write for *Soccer Australia*. Inexplicably, he seemed honoured to be asked and was happy to oblige. He faxed through his first article within a fortnight.

Twelve months later, almost everyone we could think of was contributing to the magazine. Sports reporters from *The Age*, *Sydney Morning Herald*, *The Daily Telegraph*, *The Australian* and the BBC World Service had been enlisted, as well as a few former Socceroos. Even Nigel Griggs, the bass player from Split Enz and a Liverpool fanatic, had written for us. We'd interviewed every celebrity in Australia who knew what a soccer ball was, and courtesy of Ettore's silver tongue, *Soccer Australia* now featured competitions where the first prize might be a trip to the World Cup finals in France.

Maybe more importantly, the Socceroos had half a chance of making it to the finals themselves. Who knew what that might mean for the magazine? Things were definitely on the up.

Man United

John and I used to lie awake at night plotting the future. With the room blackened, we'd imagine perfect lives ahead: what jobs we'd have, where we'd live, and, driven by the lingering inspiration of *AutoZoot*, what cars we'd own and what irresistible – possibly superfluous – accessories we'd pile them up with. Armed with an encyclopaedic knowledge of *Modern Motor*, *Auto Car* and the *American Auto Consumers Guide*, we'd agonise over whether the sports tachometer and Le Mans racing stripes could be squeezed in under the $8000 price limit we'd painstakingly negotiated.

Once we'd sorted out our wheels, we'd file through the rest of life's nagging details. On any given night, my brother might decide to be a scientist living in London with a wife and three children, driving a Pontiac TransAm with metallic paint and electric windows. But while I, for no apparent reason, thought I'd probably end up a doctor, and I vacillated between the Torana SLR and the V8 Leyland P76 – you could fit a 44-gallon drum in its famously bloated boot (perfect for medical supplies) – I was in no doubt about the city in which, in years to come, I'd be making my turbo-charged house calls: it could only be Ballarat.

The impossible allure of the Ballarat Cup had been almost enough in itself to propel the town past the likes of Paris, Rome, New York and my beloved London as the place to be. This was all well and good, but I hadn't quite taken on board the horrifying underbelly to this seemingly harmless thought – that after half a lifetime in the outback, I had, against my better judgement, become an Australian. Sort of. And worse still, a rural Australian.

A handful of years in the Wimmera–Mallee had ensured that England, and its recklessly frenetic capital city, was now well beyond my comprehension as a real-time, day-to-day place. Even Ballarat looked a little unrestrained compared to Horsham's Firebrace Street late on Saturday mornings, which was as much hullabaloo as seemed decent. To its credit, though, Ballarat had just a taste of the restless glamour of the world's major economic centres, as well as a couple of extra soccer magazines in the shops; an alluring cocktail in any man's language. The presence of western Victoria's only Kentucky Fried Chicken outlet didn't hurt.

All of the above came to mind when Mum and Dad turned *Countdown* off one Sunday evening to tell us we were leaving Horsham to live within walking distance of the Colonel. We'd moved house five times in seven years, occasionally crossing hemispheres on the way, so for us kids it was acceptably bad news. Emptying one house and filling another, and leaving a bunch of friends behind en route, seemed fair enough in my eyes. It was for Dad's work; the schools in a bigger town would be better for us. We were back in front of the telly before Gavin Wood announced the Top 10.

After a little light research I realised there was more to Ballarat than exotically stocked newsagents and crispy-skinned tubs of Kentucky. It was the second-biggest inland city in Australia – after Canberra – and, courtesy of a median strip dotted with ornamental rotundas and pastel flowerbeds, it had one of the widest main streets in the whole country. Then there was the Eureka Stockade where, during the 1850s gold rush, miners revolting against licence fees were ambushed by the military in a pre-dawn raid. Twenty-nine people died a few hundred yards from Ballarat's city centre in the event routinely described as the closest Australia has come to a civil uprising. Though Aboriginals may beg to differ.

The horrors of Eureka Stockade were a little abstract to a kid in Year 8. There was, nonetheless, a local institution to send a chill down the spine: John and I had twigged that we were on our way to St Patrick's College. And St Pat's wasn't just a school, it

was a *boarding school.* Unfortunately I'd read the books –
Tom Brown's Schooldays didn't cheer me up like I'd hoped
– and though we weren't sure exactly what lay in store,
we understood that the good times were over, 9 a.m. to
3.30 p.m. weekdays at least.

Hauling our possessions down the Avenue of
Honour, Ballarat's 14-mile tree-lined tribute to locals
who'd enlisted in World War I, we shoehorned ourselves
into our new house: cathedral-style frontage, dirt-
floor garage, child-size kitchen and all. It was suitably
eccentric after the town-dwarfing willow tree and four
back doors of the H-shaped home we'd left behind.
Once unpacked, and with the days counting down to
boarding school, all there was left to do was brood.

Day one at St Pat's and it was clear a new world
order had been established. The absence of girls lent
an austere, regimented air to the place, an edge not
softened by the requirement to call teachers 'Sir' – an
archaic, comic touch for the average country-town
blow-in. And in a darkened, church-like classroom, it
sunk in slowly that I was sitting in a building where
the ancient language of Latin was currently being
taught. If not for the jarring presence of a couple of
flourishing eucalypts, their branches batting fruitlessly
against locker doors outside, I might have migrated to
Victorian England since breakfast.

Walking friendless around St Pat's during the first
few late-summer lunchtimes – John and I had the usual

brothers' pact to ignore each other at school – I studied the musty array of black-and-white photos bordering the corridors and assembly area. This stony faced line-up of ex-pupils had achieved stuff they (and you) knew you'd never manage yourself. There was a series of first XVIII footy team photos from the 1950s, florid penmanship recording St Pat's highest score – 48 goals, 28 points to Ballarat High School's absolute zero, with a kid called John James kicking a lazy thirty-five goals. Other portraits revealed that James, as well as another boy in the front row, Brian Gleeson, had gone on to win Brownlow Medals.[12] I hadn't heard of either of them, but unless school historians were pulling a serious swifty you had to say it was kind of intimidating.

With heavy blackened wood frames almost swallowing their subjects, there was a premier of Tasmania, Test cricketers, orchestra conductors, lieutenant generals from the Boer War and beyond, even a 'world famous surgeon' (and I was quite prepared to take their word for it). With my own ambitions not stretching any further than Arsenal winning the FA Cup one day – and hopefully it being on the telly – I wasn't sure how I could compete.

These solitary laps of crowded corridors were as educational as they were demoralising, but a couple of weeks in I was saved, unexpectedly, by the Shed Oval. Notwithstanding the absence of an actual shed, this humble venue would more than deliver the goods:

for it was here I ran into Sea Monkey, Dragon, Barba, Rhino and Davies.

On a disoriented detour one sweaty Monday morning, daydreaming just for a change, I'd almost collided with a gang of Year 7s booting around, incredibly, a soccer ball. After a fortnight of submersion in St Pat's overbearing old boys, Latin declensions in dry heat and the nagging, insistent presence of the Victorian Football League, it was pleasing – like discovering penicillin must have been – to stumble onto this exotic spectacle.

Still, it took some time to insinuate my way into proceedings. But after Sea Monkey and his troupe had spent a handful of 35°C lunchtimes suspiciously eyeing the bloke with the pudding-bowl haircut and unseasonal dark-blue school blazer (I thought it made my shoulders look broader) embarking on relentless, casual laps of the oval for no apparent reason, they finally gave me the nod.

I was home at last. Especially as, amid all the soccer fans in the house, there was one true obsessive: Sea Monkey himself. Mark Seymour, a Manchester United fan and, imposingly, nudging 6 foot tall (or so it seemed) at the age of twelve, was pleased to meet someone similarly afflicted and quickly, cunningly, nicknamed me 'Arsenal'. Lacking his poetic flair, I called him Seymour.

A sharp-witted, sometimes bitterly amusing bloke,

Seymour and I gradually became friends, despite the odd obstacle – 14 or 15 inches difference in height, for starters. He'd had a difficult childhood, his parents separating when he was seven, staying in an orphanage for months at a time and now living with his mum and four-year-old brother Jason at the Welcome Stranger caravan park. Mark's was an alien world, to say the least; although, to be honest, it wasn't any more peculiar than the average Dickensian weekday at St Pat's.

Early 1977 was not the time to be a Gunners fan, and lying, confused, on my sky-blue bedspread after school most afternoons, I was beginning to conclude that Arsenal would never win a match again. Not until we moved out of Ballarat, anyway. It was eight defeats in a row since I'd started at St Pat's – somehow, from nowhere, sucking the super out of Supermac, the worst run in the Gunners' 90-year history. And in case I might forget my unfortunate birthright, there was Seymour calling me 'Arsenal' ten times a day just to drive the rusty nail in.

None of these games had been on *The Big Match*, so it was difficult to tell how badly we were playing. Terry Neill's claim after one of the losses, though, that 'We couldn't have beaten eleven dustbins' wasn't encouraging. The only saving grace was that Supermac had scored in four of the defeats, although it wasn't inconceivable he'd manage the noteworthy feat of topping the goal-scoring chart in a relegated side.

By the end of February, I could hardly look as Arsenal teetered drunkenly from one loss to another. Had they really been in the top six leading into the Iestyn fixture four months before? But on 23 March, two and a half months after we'd left Horsham, the Gunners scraped a 1–1 draw with Stoke and it seemed the Ballarat curse might be broken. I could finally stop the self-flagellation when Arsenal beat Leicester City. A frizzy-haired kid named Graham Rix scored three minutes into his debut; then another youngster, David O'Leary, who'd later endure an unfeasible six years without a league goal, got two more before ten minutes were up: 3–0 and even we couldn't lose from there. Suddenly the calm waters of eighth or ninth place were beckoning. Mid-table mediocrity. It had a lovely ring to it.

Seymour, over for the day from the caravan park, confided later that his first visit to our house had been an eye-opener. Dad was a surgeon, Mum had a lilting Irish accent, there were photos of our various priestly uncles meeting the Pope spread reverently around the living area like holy water, and, for good measure, our record player was so old it looked like it needed an ear trumpet for amplification.

There was also the engineering curiosity that stood defiantly in the garage, as strange as a Venusian spaceship at the time: my fold-out Peugeot bike. Added to that was the museum mustiness of a boys' room collapsing in soccer posters and bookshelves spilling over with *Shoot!*, *Score* and *Scorcher* football annuals, and without a traceable hint that it hadn't been transported intact earlier that day from a suburb of north London.

Thankfully, Mark was nothing if not adaptable, and in any case he was here on business. Seymour, John and I had – admittedly after little deliberation and scant research – concluded that the people of Ballarat were in dire, immediate need of an Arsenal and Manchester United supporters' magazine. Sitting in our bedroom under the watchful eye of all twenty-two first-division teams, we drew up our plans: volume one, number one – six pages. Two with photos, four with news, punchy opinions and occasional, possibly bogus, competitions. A magazine to be duplicated and photocopied half-a-dozen times by a helpful St Pat's staff member (we imagined) and then distributed to a legion of would-be soccer fans – well, six to start with – among the 800-strong population of the school. The cover price: fifteen cents; the name of the magazine, *Red 'n' White* – Arsenal and United's common colours. As the meeting adjourned we smiled at each other knowingly. This was going to be huge.

A few years either side of March '77, the three of us mightn't have been so eager to join forces. Arsenal had been English champions six years previous, while

Manchester United had won the European Cup three years before that. Seymour, though, had seen shell-shocked United slumming it in division two with the York Citys and Oxfords as recently as 1975, while these days the Gunners seemed to be perennial relegation hopefuls, so our teaming in photocopied opposition to the Great Enemy seemed a noble cause. I refer to Liverpool, who looked for all the world like they'd be unbeatable for the next decade. Their nine league championships and four European Cups in the following thirteen years would adequately bear out our worst fears.

We hacked at Mum's typewriter after school and on the next couple of weekends, setting ourselves a mid-April deadline. The text was coming along nicely, while our executive decision to shamelessly lift photos from *Shoot!* meant we had an endless supply of pictures of our idols, albeit that, once photocopied, then copied again with our handwritten captions added, through the blur you'd swear Arsenal and United played in a perpetual pea souper. Other compromises came via the erratically guillotined page edges – Id O'Leary was one casualty, Martin 'In' Buchan, another – but these were mere details. All we cared about was hitting the streets and battling it out with *Shoot!* and *Roy Of The Rovers* for our cut of the hard-earned Aussie soccer dollar.

Issue one was jam-packed. We previewed the forthcoming FA Cup semi-finals, anticipating – hold on to your hats – a Manchester United victory against Leeds, while for historians among our pubescent readership, there was, far from explicably, a look back at the 1948 FA Cup final. Still we weren't done. We'd recently discovered the revolutionary Blu-Tack and needed to spread the word. 'For all poster fans,' we wrote feverishly, 'if you don't want to ruin your best wall posters with sticky tape then get some Blu-Tack, a kind of sticky plasticine. Blu-Tack is made by Bostik and our tests with it have proved that it can replace sticky tape.' We were as excited as it sounds.

What with 1940s FA Cup match reports and creative home-decorating hints, we knew we were offering rare value for money; nonetheless the 15-cent cover price gave us a sleepless night or two. Believing some might consider it prohibitive, our editorial addressed the tough issues. We explained that photocopying costs were the main factor and rather obsessively outlined other expenses, including paper and research materials, helpfully adding that 'typewriter maintenance' shouldn't be neglected as a drain on our resources.

In the event, we'd concerned ourselves unnecessarily. Within days of release, the print run of six copies had been snapped up. A sell-out first time around: gross income ninety cents. We were up and running.

Viking for a Day

Some newspaper headlines leave you scratching for words. Like, say, *Supermac for South Melbourne*. It was the debut year of the Philips Soccer League (PSL) – Australia's first ever national club competition in any sport, it was claimed – and I'd cleared an hour or two a day in my already packed soccer schedule to get pretty het up about it.

An American sports marketing svengali might have come up with action-hero team names like Melbourne Rowdies, Sydney Sting or Canberra Blizzard. I would have given that the big thumbs-up, but was happy enough with what was on the table – a stew of clubs and cultures that made the Australian national league more or less unique in world football. Hakoah-Eastern Suburbs, St George-Budapest, Footscray JUST and Fitzroy United Alexander would be among the nation's premier soccer protagonists going into the 1977 season.

It hadn't occurred to me that mainstream Australia might struggle to cope with this goulash of ethnic tongue-twisters, even if you explained that JUST was an acronym for Jugoslav United Soccer Team, and that Alexander was a reference to Alexander the Great. I wasn't too fussed; it was mind-boggling enough that, courtesy of the 0/10 Network (soon to be become Channel 10), the *Philips Top Soccer* highlights show would be on in Ballarat *every* Saturday night of the season.

From the off, I refused to let a scrap of PSL data go unrecorded. I bought a sturdy orange cardboard folder and devoted a foolscap page to each club, noting every result, every scorer for each team and subsequent league position round by round. Not forgetting attendances, which I tallied weekly, ultimately ascertaining each club's average crowd for the year, as well as the league's overall average attendance. My maths – if not my sanity – was coming on a treat.

I was learning to love the Philips Soccer League, and the front-page Supermac scoop in *Soccer Action* cemented the relationship. Arsenal had ended the season a comfy eighth, easily their best performance since I'd gotten on board, with Malcolm Macdonald equal top scorer in the first division on twenty-five goals. Now he was jetting to Tullamarine to don the South Melbourne colours for three games, set to indoctrinate Victorians in the dual fine arts of lethal finishing and the proper cultivation of sideburns. The PSL was bewitching enough as it was – you might recall Hakoah-Eastern Suburbs enjoying a stellar campaign – but the notion of Supermac playing for a club 70 miles down the road from St Pat's ... improbably, Ron Barassi, John Edrich and the other stars of John's and my lives to date had been trumped.

Supermac's appearance at Middle Park was already shaping as the highlight of the late twentieth century; then South Melbourne's forthcoming opponents St George-Budapest announced a guest player of their own and things began to get a little blurry. It was George – Charlie George – none other than the Gunners legend himself. The two best players in Arsenal's history (if you asked me) would be facing off in an inner suburb of Melbourne for opposing Australian national league teams. It was almost eerie.

Granted, I didn't have much to compare it with, but I was more or less satisfied with the dozen years of my life so far: I'd found myself in a loving family and frequently temperate climate while the Gunners had managed to cheat relegation for three seasons straight. And on a winter's afternoon in South Melbourne I was, thanks to the visionaries behind the Philips Soccer League, reaching for the cosmos. We missed the first three minutes of the game – I'll never forgive whoever was responsible, if it wasn't me – and the ground was packed. I knew it would have to be a record PSL crowd (eclipsing the 11,300 at the Adelaide City v Western Suburbs fixture in round five, a surprise home defeat), and George had already put St George ahead, which even South Melbourne fans thought had a nice ring to it.

The old stadium – all rickety metal and wood – was rocking, and at the announcer's behest hundreds of us kids spilled onto the sidelines to spectate, within touching distance of the pitch markings. Charlie George was on the same actual continuous patch of grass as me, and on any other day I wouldn't have ignored him completely, mesmerised by the bull-necked Macdonald. Supermac pummelled home both of South Melbourne's goals, nearly sparking the most prepubescent pitch invasion of all time, twice. It was really him; *The Big Match*, FA Cups, hey, his legs *were* a bit peculiar, it's *actually him* – I might have to leave it there.

The final score of South Melbourne 2, St George 3 – ultimately neither team coming within cooee of the championship – was only a footnote. As our Renault 16 slowly rode the highway back to Ballarat, my Supermac trance lingered. Now that I'd shared breathing space with an England centre-forward, Bacchus Marsh lion park and mystical, mock-medieval Kryal Castle seemed underdone in comparison and I didn't spare them a thought as we drove past. I was more convinced than ever that *Red 'n' White* was where the real action was.

At home again and slowly recuperating, John and I had extra bounce as we pieced the next issue together at bedroom HQ. Unfathomably, with word of mouth at St Pat's our circulation had bulleted to fifteen, and even our sneakily increased price of twenty cents – hyperinflation in the typewriter-maintenance market was a killer – failed to stem the enthusiasm of our readership. And rightly so, for *Red 'n' White* was heading bravely into foreign terrain: we'd introduced a letters page.

In the spirit of a democratic age, the lines had been thrown open to the hitherto-muzzled Catholic teenage soccer fans of Ballarat in issue three, and the couple of Manchester United enthusiasts at school grappled with the lone Liverpool supporter. It had the potential to get nasty, with neither 'A Keegan fan' nor '3 United supporters, Ballarat' holding back; we were all grateful for the calming presence of one 'Mark Seymour, United fan (with brains)', who, uncannily, had the same name as the Red Devils representative in our editorial team.

We also initiated a look at the Ballarat scene, analysing the state of all the junior soccer pitches in town. 'How have the grounds managed under the tread of 22 feet every Sunday?' we asked, not caring for the usual quota of two legs per player. Frequently temperate climate aside, it had actually been the worst winter in the area for years, and our assessment that, 'If Ballarat went for, say two weeks without rain or snow all these pitches would be really good,' wasn't meant to be funny.

The snow report was dear to *Red 'n' White* hearts, with both Mark and I lining up each week in the St Pat's green, white and blue. Not having played a proper match since Buster had bent my left leg in two back in

Horsham, I'd been queasy about re-entering the fray, especially the cauldron of Ballarat junior soccer. To a degree, I'd emerged from my plaster cast a broken man, with cowering – more than ever – a key aspect of my game plan. Additionally, with my Wimmera flaws I knew I'd be battling to make it on the grand stage, but despite it all I couldn't help myself. I was pathologically focused during the pre-season, hoofing the ball around for hours a day with John, Mark, both, or just the punch-drunk plasterboard wall of our garage. And persistence in the face of cold, hard facts surely counted for something.

Seymour, all nigh-on 6 foot of him, was intimidating enough with his sheer verticality, and he even headed the ball with his eyes open: gold dust. Other key men were Grant Davies, our Blu Tack-gloved keeper; Paul 'Rhino' Ryan – a devout, bespectacled, but suicidally tough defender; Paul 'Dragon' Drohan, our Olympian winger, and Dominic Barba, a fast-footed Mediterranean born for a shiny-suited role in *Saturday Night Fever*. If our training manoeuvres were any indication, we'd take some beating in season '77.

Sadly, they proved to be no indication whatsoever. We won a game here and there, overturning Wendouree Wanderers with imperious ease, but sent packing by Creswick the following weekend. For my part I was off the pace, my inherent shortness exacerbated by the sudden onset of puberty throughout the Ballarat league. It had gone through the place like a dose of salts and every second opponent seemed to be 4 inches taller overnight, nursing a half-decent mo and sounding a little like Frank Thring.[13] I was thirteen now, and being left behind.

It was the end of an Arctic soccer campaign and I'd clung to my place in the St Pat's line-up despite chronic goallessness. The final game of the season was against lowly Sebastopol Vikings and I was desperate to notch my first ever goal in the major leagues. Naturally I didn't, but there were compensations. The match was like any other that year, with me contributing the odd neat pass here, the odd miskick there, and a squibbed tackle wherever necessary, but in the second half, with St Pat's a goal or two to the good, a strange thing happened.

It was an unimportant moment. The ball was played towards me at the halfway line, with a Viking, possibly bearded, hot on my heels. I'd spent the season being kicked out of games, balloon-lightweight and not near enough a wizard of the dribble to compensate. But in this slow-motion microsecond, I dropped my shoulder, let the ball run through my legs and turned to regain possession, leaving the defence split, my unshaven opponent careering into the space I'd vacated, and me looking – for the only time in my life – like a footballing genius. It was, if I do say so myself, a nifty piece of skill.

The entire Vikings team stood and applauded. Our coach was too shocked to speak. Mark and Dominic Barba had to pick their jaws up from the turf before they could join the attack, and the chance went begging. Did I care? I hardly got a kick for the rest of the match I was that dazed, replaying my Pele moment. The next season was six months away. I had a memory to sustain me for as long as it took.

In June, two announcements had caught my eye. First, that we were off to England, mainly to celebrate my grandparents' sixtieth wedding anniversary. Then, in an almost simultaneous telex, the Australian Soccer Federation unveiled a four-team tournament featuring the Socceroos, Red Star Belgrade, Celtic of Scotland and – wow – Arsenal. It was too much. The untoppable Supermac v Charlie George epic was to be cast aside by Supermac himself and the actual Gunners XI, live in Australia. But my excitement was snuffed out in a breath, with all our matches cruelly scheduled for Sydney and Adelaide. A brisk 400- or 600-mile drive interstate wasn't an option: the games might as well have been at Wembley, or Jupiter. Knowing I'd be within 5 miles of Arsenal's home ground a few weeks later, though, wasn't a bad pick-me-up.

There was housekeeping to attend to before we left for the UK: a mooted *Red 'n' White* package tour to Melbourne. The final of the international tournament,

a couple of days after John and I would land at
Heathrow, had been a magnet for our entrepreneurial
leanings and issue three trumpeted the strictly limited
offer, written as officiously as we could to impress our
friends' parents: 'From the Melbourne bus terminal a
taxi will take the party to Olympic Park. At the ground
the party will take position to see the game from seats
in the stadium previously booked. Return shall be by
train. At the time of print, the cost of this amazing
tour is less than fifteen dollars.' Regrettably the tour –
unnecessarily lavish taxi trip to Olympic Park and all
– failed to eventuate, with Mark's mum refusing to let
him go to the city that day. There were no refunds;
fortunately, there were also no takers.

Despite losing two-thirds of the editorial team
for eight weeks, *Red 'n' White* stopped for no man.
We'd decided – albeit with no conceivable alternative
– to leave the operation solely in Seymour's control.
Responsibility for this burgeoning enterprise was a
heavy burden for a lone twelve-year-old, our grand
ambitions encapsulated on the cover of the latest issue.
With the price anchored at twenty cents, the tell-tale
phrase wasn't far away. UK: 7½ pence.

Looking through a Grilled Onion

It was some time between Turkey and Switzerland that the captain made the announcement: Geoff Boycott, in his first game for his country since 1974, had run out Derek Randall and England was 5 for 82 against Australia. The plane rocked with nasally, sleepy cheers – evidence, I thought, that not everyone on our British Airways flight to London was actually British.

In the two and a half years since the legendary but forgetful John Edrich had neglected his PR obligations and left a Wimmera youngster hanging on the telephone, I'd lost a little of my English fervour. But trapped in an economy seat armed only with my imagination, picturing a thicket of moustaches and open chests, pendants flying around necks and broad Aussie accents telling Pommy batsmen to nick off back to the pavilion, I knew it'd be a while yet before I'd be asking Mum to ring up about Australian citizenship.

Maybe I'd never live in England again, but it was still home. A nation that knew a jumper was a pullover and a thong a flip-flop: these would always be my people. And anywhere in the UK was dazzling, including Pearson's in Enfield, so I was happy to be buried neck-deep in replica soccer shirts in their sports-apparel department within twenty-four hours of landing.

I shelled out a reasonable percentage of Dad's weekly wage, leaving Pearson's coated with a 100 per cent nylon aroma that lingered for months and a bag containing the England football team's shirt, shorts and socks. The luridly candy stripes on the shirt sleeves and nappyish plastic of the shorts failed to wipe the girlish glee from my face. I was ready for the major event now, and in full England kit I'd have to make the best-dressed list at my grandparents' diamond wedding anniversary.

John and I were a couple of years beyond our altar-boy heyday, but within the prevailing spirit of pomp, and being very, *very* many thousands of miles from anyone in Ballarat's key twelve-to-fourteen age bracket who'd have cacked themselves at the sight, we agreed to don the vestments one last time for Grandma and Grandad's celebratory Mass. As the only male guests able to fit into the robes, though, we were pretty much cornered.

With dozens of relatives over from Ireland and across the UK for the event, the streets of Enfield were like a family photo album. But in the summer of '77 the rest of England wasn't so pullover cosy, and another Arsenal fan with Irish roots had to take a share of the blame. Johnny Rotten and his fellow Sex Pistols had been rubbing lots of people up the wrong way during the previous twelve months.

In a ceremonial bonanza, 1977 also marked the silver jubilee of the coronation of Queen Elizabeth, and amid the royal festivities – there were Union Jacks hanging off newspaper pages, buildings, any available space – the Sex Pistols released 'God Save The Queen'. Workers at the CBS record pressing plant threatened to strike, but the song ultimately reached number two in the charts. The band's major crime, other than appearing to call Her Majesty a moron on a hit single, was to drop a four-letter word or two on prime-time television. After putting a boot through his TV in disgust, a Welsh bus driver captured the mood of an angry populace. 'I swear with the best of them,' he said, 'but I'm not having it on my telly.'

I could boast a healthy interest in popular music – my brother's collection of Wings and Chicago records had ensured this was the case – but I spent endless hours listening to BBC Radio without so much as hearing the name of Johnny's group. They'd been banned from the airwaves and, in any case, songs about H-bombs, fascist regimes and the IRA were unlikely to strike much of a chord, so punk passed me by. But if I'd known that Johnny Rotten had a 'Go Go Gunners' poster on the sitting-room wall of his West Brompton

squat, 'God Save The Queen' might have had a ghost
of a chance of supplanting 'If You Leave Me Now'
from my personal hit parade.

Anarchy on the streets aside, my brother and I
were uneasy under the weight of three generations of
family history, about a thousand years of undistilled
Catholicism all told, present at St George's church
on the diamond day. Showing signs of ring rust we
dealt indecisively with the cruets and altar bell, but
after a creaky rendition of our gospel, offertory and
Eucharistic responsibilities, we sighed from beneath
the vestments as the priest, Uncle Den, signalled the
end of the Mass (or 'Mah-ss', as he preferred) with a
caped, broad-shouldered flourish.

Our uncle, who'd sealed a place in our hearts by
heading the 1973 *Guinness Book of Records* expedition,
and who'd recently lost every hair on his head and
brow after contracting an obscure disease back in
Rhodesia, joined the procession to the official party
at Grandma and Grandad's a mile up the road. It was
a long, relentlessly Irish night. As both Dad's parents
had migrated from Ireland as young adults, naturally
the piano took a pounding as the Gaelic folklore rang
out around their hedge-fronted home. This was real
Irish music; nothing someone like me, a veteran only
of K-Tel's *40 Sing-along Shamrock Favourites*, would
have known. I changed from my altar-boy best to my
iridescent England kit, an Anglo infiltrator in a Celtic

stronghold, and had a whale of a time.

My grandparents' party, however, wasn't the quirkiest event on the Enfield calendar that summer. In an eccentric suburb, home to Guinness' records and whose cricket side had once fielded local tearaway Boris Karloff as an opening bowler, it was little surprise that when poring over the fine print of Grandad's *Telegraph* one morning, I discovered that Enfield Football Club, which competed in the equivalent of the English fifth or sixth division, had a game lined up the following day: against the national team of Kuwait.

Enfield v Kuwait would have been must-see entertainment under most circumstances, but given that Australia was due to play the Kuwaitis later in the year in World Cup qualifiers, it was the only show in town. The next evening, about a thousand Enfield fans were there in the leafy August dusk to witness a strange prelude to a nine-month campaign against the likes of Barking, Tooting & Mitcham and Dulwich Hamlet; their north London heroes – all of whom had day jobs, probably – versus the cream of the oil-rich Middle East.

Any football match I could witness in the flesh was enthralling, even a pre-season friendly between two pretty ordinary teams. So at half-time, after forty-five minutes of looking into the whites of the eyes of *real soccer players* – a title that, for me, crossed the great Arab/cockney divide – I was having one of the ten best evenings of my life. The 0–0 score line – and, as in

Shakespeare's Footeball Joke Book, both teams were lucky to score nil – only meant the game was still agonisingly in the balance.

During the break I skipped to the kiosk to buy the cheese-and-onion crisps and the middle-aged bloke behind the counter muttered dryly, 'You've come a long way for this game, son.' I took the crisps and smiled politely, assuming he'd confused me with someone who'd come a long way for the game. It took a minute to register – the first time I'd ever been accused outright of having an Australian accent. It had been eight years, but I knew – and under a few hundred watts' interrogation I might have admitted it – that I didn't sound like I was from England anymore. This was as bad as it got, though; someone who'd know telling me I wasn't English. The cheese and onion stuck in my craw.

It was an unusual hour and a half. On the one hand I was in the UK to stock up on Englishness, to grab as many memories as I could, like I was on *Supermarket Spree*, to sustain me till adulthood. But I'd been following the Australian soccer team since 1974 and I was at least as keen a fan of them as England. I spent the second half studiously assembling a dossier on the Kuwaitis for future Socceroo reference, as Enfield ultimately won more easily than the 1–0 result suggested. Slurs notwithstanding, it had been a good day. And the Socceroos were, I noted sagely, heading for a second consecutive World Cup finals …

•

Supporting an English football team in Australia meant they were yours – you didn't have to share them with anyone. Also, whether you liked it or not you were barricaded from the tribal side of the game. I relied on *Shoot!* for cultural analysis, oblivious to it being, in the nervously sanitised world of children's magazines, a sort of junior-soccer *Pravda*. But out on the streets there were, for instance, plenty of Tottenham Hotspur fans who *despised* Arsenal, not least because the Gunners had somehow, unprecedentedly, been elected into the first division at Spurs' expense – back in 1919, mind you – after they'd finished in a lowly fifth place in the second division. The small matter of the Great War having split the two seasons in question didn't seem to quell Tottenham's ire.

Meanwhile, further to the north, Leeds and Manchester United loathed each other for all sorts of reasons, theoretically traceable to the War of the Roses in 1455. These, and dozens of other rivalries up and down the country, ensured that being a soccer fan in England linked you – either in love or hate, nearly always hate – with millions of people within three or four hours drive.

In Horsham, if you were an Aussie-rules supporter there was a packed classroom shaping your view of your team and the game. You'd develop a sense of what kind of people barracked for each club – fat kids liked Richmond – and being a fan of a team marked you out as a member of whichever gang. For me, though, oblivious to the hatreds and passions underpinning English football, following the Gunners was as personal and intimate as collecting cigarette cards or antique teapots, without fear of infiltration from the outside world.

But in August 1977, John's and my little secret was about to be blown wide open: we were on our way to our first Arsenal game. I'd waited almost half my life for this: a summery evening, as Dad, Uncle Shawn, John and I walked down Avenell Road towards Highbury. I'd sweated over the results of a couple of hundred Gunners matches, painstakingly analysing scraps of information about each player, computing results week by week by week, wasting entire afternoons at school designing futuristic Arsenal kits, imagining new signings (what if Best, Keegan, Currie, Worthington, Toshack or Mervyn Day joined the club?), seeing three or four Arsenal goals a season on *The Big Match*, sketching them from memory in a drawing pad and seeing them in my dreams for months: there were never enough hours in a day.

All those years of dedication seemed to culminate here – there was the East Stand, which had nearly bankrupted the club in the 1930s, looming like the Sphinx – but with thousands of Gunners fans bearing down on us from every direction, there were more urgent matters at hand than imbibing the beauty of the moment. I'd never seen so many people; big people, grown-up people, clearly unafraid to plough us down if they must. I sucked in my shoulders and hunkered down, loving every minute of it.

To be honest, with all the effort I'd put in – 1974–77 inclusively – I had a vague notion that people should have looked a little more pleased to see me than they did. As it was, amid the waves of north London accents, red-and-white scarves and clumps of Arsenal badges pinned to coat pockets, all lightly scented with beef burgers and grilled onions – smells I'd associate with Highbury for decades to come – I was overwhelmed by the idea that almost everyone I could see (or *sense*, at least; I could hardly see a thing) was fanatical about the same team as I was. I'd never been in a cluster of more than five even lukewarm Arsenal supporters.

It was the first home game of the season against Everton, who might easily be better than we were. I'd expected to be jumpier than I was, though, having coped less than admirably with my previous live Arsenal experience, via Iestyn's short-wave radio. But this evening the stress was spread among the 33,000 of us, and despite my deep-sleep panic attack last time around I was, somehow, basically looking forward to the match.

And this wasn't just another fixture: there was history in the offing. Pat Jennings, probably the most celebrated goalkeeper in the league, was making his home debut for Arsenal. Despite hair so hedge-thick and lustrous he might have been mistaken for one of the older Osmonds, the 32-year-old had been eased out the door by Tottenham a few weeks earlier. Concluding that he was ever so marginally over the hill, Spurs had offloaded their legendary keeper for loose change: £40,000. Jennings, one of half-a-dozen Irishmen in our first XI, would play more than three hundred games for Arsenal and captain Northern Ireland at the World Cup finals at the age of forty-one. Tottenham, one is tempted to conclude, had made a slight misjudgement.

We sat in the West Stand and focused on *everything*: the crowd rocking and billowing in the North Bank; the rumble of thousands of people chanting and clapping, each song swirling, peaking then washed over by the next; feeling, in the upper tier, both infinitely closer and miles further away than watching it on *The Big Match*. All backed by the awesome thought that we'd be absolutely equal first on the planet to witness Pat Jennings' home debut for the club.

A week later, I'd reached sensory overkill. Urged on by a stand liberally populated with Gunners fans who sounded like Harold Steptoe and Blakey from *On the Buses*, Arsenal had beaten Everton 1–0, with Jennings' hair rarely agitated as he watched the evening unfold at the other end of the ground. Supermac's sideys got more of a workout as we'd pegged the Evertonians back. Despite the score line, my deaf uncle – it was weird to think he'd experienced every Arsenal match he'd been to in the last forty years in pure silence – had patiently explained where the Gunners were going wrong: more or less everywhere, apparently.

Seven days later, there was no-one to set John and myself straight. Brilliantly, we were at Highbury again, this time for the second round of the League Cup against – stone the crows – Manchester United. The seating arrangements had been tampered with and tickets for our regular haunt, the West Stand, were sold out, so Dad and Uncle Shawn headed for the North Bank behind one of the goals, familiar terrain for both either side of World War II. But rather than being surrounded by the previous week's much-loved sitcom characters, John and I had been posted elsewhere. Ours were tickets for the Arsenal boarding school.

We were cattle-prodded into the sinister-sounding Boys' Enclosure, a kind of detention centre for under-14s. Taking our place with hundreds of other abandoned pre-pubescents, and separated from our family by ten thousand or so Arsenal supporters (we thought we spotted Dad and Uncle Shawn – about ninety degrees and three hundred rows away), we were a little anxious as to whether there were any of those infamous soccer hooligans about. A sea of shrill boyish voices piercing the night sky with 'Oh come on, Arsenal', and 'Hugh, stop pushing or I'll give you a thump', gradually allayed our worst fears.

Herded in and isolated, there was a major consolation: Arsenal v Manchester United. Enfield and Kuwait locking horns had held a certain charm, but this was something else. We were talking about the second round of the League Cup here, just the last sixty-four clubs in the knockout competition. Okay, so maybe it wasn't a cast-iron nail-biter, but it was one of only three chances we had to claim a trophy in the next whole year.

In a decent replica of the Everton win, we scored near half-time to make it 1–0 – the goal by Supermac after a blunder by In Buchan – but everything else was like the Twilight Zone. From our near-subterranean vantage point, the whole stadium seemed bent out of shape. Being almost at boot level *Arsenal* and *United* suddenly became real people, like you might see at the shops, but floodlit, in shorts, and shouting at each other. When the ball was on our touchline, with players ambling, riding a tackle or winding up for a throw-in, you could hear them grunt and see the sweat on their arms. It was absolutely amazing.

The tune of the World War II favourite 'Quartermaster's Store' came in waves, as thousands of Arsenal fans, swearing like Sex Pistols, taunted one of the United stars: 'A shot, A miss, As weak as *@!*#@ piss, Gordon Hill, Gordon Hill', while, as I grinned and nodded excitedly, Gary Glitter also got a look-in, with a pounding chant of 'Hello, hello, Su-per-mac's back, Su-per-mac's back'.

Arsenal won a tense, but fantastic match 3–2, with Jennings' baseball-mitt hands fending off the Red Devils and our ascendant Irish midfield star Liam Brady belting one in with the outside of his foot from 20 yards. Supermac scored twice, the second after running half the length of the ground, dribbling past the United goalkeeper and rolling the ball into the net as the crowd in the North Bank went mad. Too exciting for words.

My first trip back to England had been a homecoming after a four-year aberration at the end of the Earth. Now, though, I had responsibilities elsewhere: western Victoria was actually where I lived, and with *Red 'n' White* flourishing, oddly it seemed to me I belonged back in Australia, albeit permanently reminiscing about being English. A few weeks in the UK, nonetheless, had got the creative juices in a spin. By the time we boarded the plane to Australia a few days after the vanquishing of United, John and I were already hatching a plan. Well, John was.

Unofficialdom

My brother had gone straight to the top. With my solemn consent, a bureaucratic letter – the best we could muster, anyway, no ruled lines – had been rifled off within hours. The recipient of John's urgent missive was Arsenal FC, to whom it may concern. Our mission: to establish an Australian branch of the Arsenal supporters' club.

With the proton energy boost of several real-life weeks in the northern hemisphere, the magnetic cling of England was strong. Nonetheless we were definitely back in Ballarat – just turn on the telly and BTV-6's scarily gruff newsreader Arthur Scuffins, and knockabout Fred Fargher's haphazard variety show *Six Tonight*, would bring you down to earth soon enough – so it was a blessing to have *Red 'n' White* to come home to.

In our absence, Seymour had assembled and published the latest edition. Given that it had taken the three of us to produce the much-lauded issues one to four, his solo flight had been impressive, not least his handling of our first ever competition. In the previous issue, readers had been invited to pick an Arsenal/ Manchester United superteam comprising players from our 1976/77 squads. We'd finished eighth and sixth respectively, so 'superteam' may have been pushing it, but the hype couldn't halt a flood of entries: two.

The prize was a couple of posters of the teams – both, some would later claim, with a suspiciously photocopied-several-times look about them. Petty jealousy aside, however, there could only be one winner, and that man, Seymour announced, was Dominic Barba, coincidentally star striker for the St Patrick's College juniors.

Mark's exclusive interview with the triumphant reader followed:

> R+W: What does it feel like to win our competition?
> DB: It feels real good to win something for once.
> R+W: How did you pick the correct team?
> DB: Well, I thought you would pick the six best from each side, so then I wrote them down.
> R+W: How did you know about the competition?
> DB: Mark Seymour told me that it was 'A great competition', so I thought I would give it a go, as it only cost 20 cents.

•

Genuine good news stories are hard to find. Yet here, Dominic Barba was the elated owner of a couple of indistinct, greyish, limited-edition soccer posters he might proudly display to his grandchildren, while *Red 'n' White* had brazenly pocketed a 40-cent boost to our cash reserves. It has to be said, however, that this windfall failed to excite us as it might have a few months before, for these days our sights were on a grander prize.

With all three of us together again, there was revolution in the air. We'd deduced that although *Red 'n' White* had the local Arsenal and United demographic – let's be honest – sewn up, we were shunning the devotees of nigh on ninety clubs. Could we be doing more for our public? The solution was brash: a whole new football publication for country Victoria. Its name: *League Leader.*

Thus, on 25 September 1977, the corridors of St Pat's echoed with adrenaline – among almost fifteen of its 800 students, anyway – as our athletic readership raced to claim their copy of the inaugural *League Leader (incorporating Red 'n' White)*: its hand-drawn cover star being, for no apparent reason, Derby County's not-overly-interesting midfielder Bruce Rioch. Eerily, though there's no glory in it, eighteen years later Rioch was appointed Arsenal manager and our premonition was finally, thrillingly, revealed.

Be that as it may, the focus of *League Leader* issue one was on our desperate, gritted-teeth attempts at neutrality. The most flamboyant of these came as, out of left field, we boldly (and incorrectly) tipped Seymour's arch-rivals Manchester City to win the championship – well, they'd finish fourth – with Arsenal and United nowhere in sight; scraping into the top six and eight respectively. This was harder for Mark than it was for his milder-mannered colleagues and we didn't want to push him too far. So, later in the magazine, his dash done, Seymour let rip.

United's European Cup Winners' Cup match against the French team St Etienne happened to catch his eye. After a tense 1–1 draw, fighting had erupted between rival fans, sufficiently ferocious that, sensationally – and briefly – United was thrown out of the competition. Seymour's *League Leader* opinion piece was emotionally raw and unashamedly ungrammatical. 'Whose fans deliberately took wine bottles and rotten bread rolls to this game?' Mark demanded – leaving no doubt as to whose fans did – under a headline that couldn't contain his anger: 'The French Fighted and Blamed United'.

But it had been an anxious month for the entire editorial team. Our generous Arsenal supporters' club offer appeared to have fallen upon deaf ears and, as weeks passed without return mail, John and I had to consider the possibility that one of the world's pre-eminent soccer clubs mightn't be terribly enthused at handing the PR for the franchise on this continent over to a couple of fervent – maybe dangerously – thirteen and fourteen-year-olds.

We'd almost consigned the supporters' club folly to our conceptual dustbin – alongside such failures as the short-lived *Supermacgazine* – when we were greeted after school one afternoon by a parcel that stopped us in our tracks. The size of an encyclopaedia, it was caked in stamps with Queen's heads on them and had an Arsenal crest in the top right-hand corner. Even unopened, it was the most exciting piece of mail we'd ever received.

A few weeks earlier my brother and I had been there among the onions and we were transported back again. *Six Tonight* slipped into insignificance as, like awed archaeologists, we uncovered our find. It was pages and pages of Arsenal history, player profiles, league positions, trophies won, all with the official letterhead as proof of authenticity, and all in a scratchy font that suggested they'd typed it up especially for us. To top it off, Mr Ken Friar – an Arsenal powerbroker whose name routinely appeared in the almost biblical *Rothmans Football Yearbook* – had sent a covering letter. He said 'hello', adding that he'd forwarded our request to Mr R Jones at the official Arsenal Supporters' Club. He concluded by wishing us 'all the best'.

As far as letters go, it wasn't exactly Flaubert. To us, though, it was lovely as a sonnet and we were floating as we waited for news from R Jones. Shortly afterwards, Mr Jones wrote to let us know the matter had been discussed at committee level and they'd decided Australia was too far away to stay in regular contact: so the answer was no. My brother and I looked at each other as we slowly digested the information. The two of us had been discussed at *committee level. Committee level!* We'd planted a flag on the moon.

With the absolute failure of our quest buried in an overwhelming sense of achievement, there was a solitary hurdle left to overcome in the matter: passing on the grim news to our readership. Those in the *League Leader* inner circle had gotten wind of the supporters' club plan, and would be itching to know if we could now, triumphantly, dub ourselves official. Our editorial, 'We're not Official,' laid it bare. The piece was written by the three of us and, after painstakingly outlining the flow of mail across the equator, concluded with a melancholy signature: 'The Arsenal and Man United supporters club committee (unofficial Ballarat and district branch)'.

Despite the bad tidings we were determined to finish on an upbeat note. After presciently mentioning that readers should 'look after this copy because if you keep it long enough it may become a collector's item', we thought it best to add, 'then again it might not, so don't worry about it'. But with an eye always on the future, and with, we hoped, many rainforests' worth of *League Leader* to come, we signed off cheerily: 'We hope that you enjoy this magazine and cough up 20c for next month's issue'.

Part IV

Age of Consent

It was June 1997 when Laurie Schwab passed away. The soccer writer for *The Age* six days a week for nearly three decades, and a forthright correspondent for *Soccer Australia* since before Sam's and my time, his death brought Victorian soccer to a standstill. Laurie and I had got along well, and although I'd disagreed with roughly half his opinions in both publications, basically I'd been in awe of him for as long as I could remember. He'd written virtually every word I'd ever read about the local game in the newspaper I'd relied on for Arsenal results since I was ten years old. His funeral service was like a history of soccer in Australia.

There was a respectful mourning period; then a bit of a scramble. There might only have been a dozen people in Melbourne interested in succeeding Laurie at *The Age*, but they were *very* interested. In the world of Aussie soccer – which traditionally paid peanuts, if it paid at all – *The Age* job was a major appointment. People I spoke to were surprised I wasn't putting my hand up, but frankly, I knew my limitations: experience

– not much; appetite for day-to-day, digging-up-the-dirt journalism – even less. I had a distinct, undeserved advantage over everyone else, though: insider trading.

The sports editor of the Sunday edition of the paper knew people who knew me, and before you could whisper 'nepotism' I'd been offered a part-time post with *The Sunday Age*. It was a couple of days a week, a feature article, a match preview plus whatever soccer story might break on the Saturday: infinitely less daunting than being the six-day-a-week successor to a 30-year veteran. Leaving the Spencer Street office of *The Age* on a wintry afternoon after signing on the dotted line, it was hard to believe that in eighteen months, from a standing start, I'd become an actual professional journalist. It felt like a nifty sleight of hand.

In mid-1997, Australian soccer was in uncharted territory. Terry Venables, fresh from leading England to the semi-finals of the European Championships, had recently been appointed coach of the Socceroos. The charismatic Venables, who'd been one of the hilarious stars – along with host Terry Mancini – of the Christmas edition of *The Big Match* back in the '70s – had also taken Barcelona to the final of the European Cup, and was one of the most prominent coaches in the world. His appointment was a staggeringly ambitious act by the usually cash-poor Australian soccer authorities, the Englishman being hired on a wage package maybe five or ten times more lucrative than his predecessor

Eddie Thomson. The gamble seemed to pay off as the Socceroos immediately won ten games on the trot. Come November, suddenly the only obstacle between Australia and a place in the World Cup finals was the mysterious 'an Asian team'.

Amid an unprecedented wave of publicity for what was allegedly a minor sport, the home leg of the tie against the as-yet-undetermined Asians was set for the Melbourne Cricket Ground. The first-ever official Socceroos international at the stadium, launched with an overcrowded media conference there in a wood-lined, nineteenth-century room, was also my newspaper debut. As I introduced myself to passers-by as 'the soccer reporter from *The Sunday Age*', I felt sure I was going to be exposed as a sham – *Isn't that the kid who does those Ron and Terry Dodgers cartoons?* – but somehow I mingled unnoticed with Australian soccer heavyweights and other sporting figures wheeled in from the AFL and cricket world for the day.

Soccer seemed to be moving into the big time, with Eddie McGuire, future president of the most popular Aussie Rules football club in the country and soon-to-be ubiquitous host of every TV show this side of *Mass for You At Home*, materialising as MC of the event, and I would have been basking in the reflected excitement of it all, had it not been for a minor detail: the dates of the two World Cup matches, 22 and 29 November. It could have been any other day of the week, instead it was consecutive Saturdays. Match reports: in *The Sunday Age*. Deadlines: tight. In the firing line: me.

The Age had spared every expense. Apparently deciding their Sunday soccer guru didn't need to be on the spot in Tehran amid a pulsating crowd of 128,000 manic Iranian men – females were barred from the stadium – they set me up at the office in Melbourne with a chair, a desk, a TV screen and a couple of beers. Although, credit where it's due, they didn't supply the beers.

It was a strange evening. Michael Hutchence had died earlier in the day and you could feel a certain regret in the air. For some of us the possible suicide of a youngish Australian dug closer to the bone than the death of the semi-mythical Princess Diana a few weeks before. Near kick-off time, 11 p.m., my friend and sub-editor Mick Epis, who'd spoken at length to the INXS singer the previous week, discovered that his 'final interview' had been snapped up by the *News of the World*. The British tabloid paid him a preposterous sum, then only used one quote, creating possibly a dollars-per-word world record. The couple of beers on my desk were courtesy of Mick.

The compassionate powers of alcohol might have helped me forget my main problem; that like every other non-Iranian in Australia, I had only the faintest idea who played for the Gulf nation. We'd known for just a handful of days – after Japan had snatched the penultimate finals place in a play-off – that Iran would be facing the Socceroos, and with information about the Iranians trickling through like it was classified, I hardly knew who played where, or who wore what number. Only slightly panicking, I'd arranged earlier in the evening for Sam to tape the TV preamble to the match, then replay and freeze-frame the Iran XI. A couple of minutes in, he called to dictate the results. Okay, it wasn't quite Tyleresque preparation, but thanks to Sam I knew for sure that the greying Mohammed Khakpour wore the number 4. Now I was ready for anything.

In spite of Mick's beers, it was an anxious ninety minutes for myself and the Socceroos; eleven lonely Australians in among the most intimidating crowd in world football, the rookie journalist swimming through the Ali Daeis, Azizis and Ahmadreza Abedzadehs in trying to compile an authoritative match report. It ended 1–1, nineteen-year-old Harry Kewell silencing – literally – an eighth of a million Iranians at the Azadi Stadium with an early goal. I finished my piece and sent it through to the sub-editors: 1 a.m. Knowing it would only be seen by those *Age* readers who got the late, late, late edition of the paper, I hadn't felt under too much pressure. I finished my second beer and looked around the near-empty office. The real test was yet to come.

Cadets Just the Way It Is

ABBA – The Album was playing as our publishing empire crumbled. John was off to boarding school – Xavier College in Melbourne; his idea, incredibly – but it was only with his three drawers empty and Mum issuing last-minute instructions on how many sheets were required to make a bed (well, I certainly didn't know) that the ramifications began to sink in.

The Swedish supergroup's 'Thank You for the Music' had rung around the lounge room all day from our ancient record player. It was muted by a half-closed front door as we waved to the Renault backing out the driveway, with John, his luggage, innocence and editorial expertise in tow. Late on a dry summer afternoon I had the boys' bedroom to myself, whether I liked it or not.

John's exodus to Xavier had been mooted for most of 1977, but I'd pretty much managed to block it out. It was going to be a difficult year now adjusting to life on my own, and while John and I had assiduously avoided each other during school hours for years – as per The Pact – elsewhere he'd been like a brother to me. Professionally I'd miss him too, for naturally he'd had to tender his resignation at *League Leader*. A transitional period was inevitable, as without John the magazine would no longer be burdened by the orthodoxy of graphic design, proofreading or, indeed, quality control of any description.

While my brother's departure was a blow to the solar plexus of the local soccer scene, John being the obvious brains of the operation, there was still a little brawn back at the coalface. But as Mark and I began planning our pared-back future as a two-man team – a switch from A4 to the more modest A5 pages, and writing really big, were among the measures proposed – there was a further crisis, this one terminal. The announcement was as brief as it was brutal: Seymour's family was moving to England.

Mark's mum, weary of life in Ballarat and with better work prospects overseas, was taking him and his younger brother to the UK. She and Jason would fly over first on a scouting mission, and once they'd settled in, Mark would be summoned. He was rapt: me, less so.

I could hardly believe it. With Seymour leaving and John off at boarding school, my world had caved in. Over the course of a few weeks I'd lose my two best friends, soccer kickabout partners and co-publishers, while *League Leader* had been dealt a deathblow. The

only people I ever really talked to – 90 per cent of the
time about soccer, admittedly – were cheerily exiting
my day-to-day life. And had anyone consulted me?

Despite my problems, ironically it was Seymour
who had more to complain about. With his mum and
brother heading to the UK, he'd been placed in the
care of the St Patrick's College boarding system, and
for someone inclined towards rebellion at the best of
times, the life of an inmate was never going to be a snug
fit. Months, maybe weeks, away from the adventure
of a lifetime in England, Mark was cooped up in a
dormitory with thirty other boys, presided over by
the authoritarian Brother Zoch, with midweek 7 a.m.
Masses and confessions like clockwork. He'd visit us
on Saturdays or Sundays, in full tie and blazer uniform
in accordance with college rules, with a bag of casual
clothes he was permitted to change into ten seconds
after he was off the premises. The bureaucracy drove
him up the wall. Each miserable in ways the other
couldn't contemplate, Seymour and I pressed on with
League Leader, waiting for the phone call from England
that would kill the magazine.

If 1978 wasn't shaping up badly enough already, there
was another cloud looming in first term: conscription.
For St Patrick's had a cadet program, compulsory for
Year 9s. And as far as I was concerned it was a fate
worse than boarding school.

The most striking sight during my first few weeks at St Pat's had been the appearance of the Year 9 kids every second Tuesday. It was the fortnightly cadet day, in which all 150 boys in the form came to school dressed in army uniform for an afternoon spent learning to march, salute and master generally the dullest aspects of playing soldiers.

To anyone from, say, London, Swan Hill or Horsham, it might have seemed bizarre that cadets would casually walk around town before and after school like a fourteen-year-old Middle East peacekeeping force. And because St Pat's had had cadets for decades, the sight of a cherubic five footer in full army garb didn't rate a second glance on Sturt Street.

I didn't know much about cadets, but I knew I wanted out. Being a modest 4 feet 7 inches – approximately 150th vertically out of 150 – I was at a distinct disadvantage in the more physical peer-group activities. So it was unhelpful that almost all modes of communication among thirteen to fourteen-year-old males had something of a muscular component. Nearly every recess and lunchtime there was an arm wrestle, a Chinese burn, a red gut, or a decent kicking going on in at least one corner of the school.

I'd managed to camouflage myself to the point of invisibility; quiet, semi-intelligent but not ostentatiously, and a permanent resident of the second row in class, never the first. Even my haircut, pudding-bowl perfect, was designed to pass wholly without comment. With a clean bill of neutrality to my name, I could just about afford to be the class's resident *wogball* fanatic.

There'd been only the one slip-up in fifteen months or so. I'd found a pair of Leeds United socks in a sports store in Mair Street early in the year – a major coup, even for an Arsenal fan – and decided to wear them to soccer training after school the next day. I'd always thought of socks as being like underwear, that if you played your cards right no-one but your mum need be any the wiser, but I hadn't allowed for the half-inch I'd grown in the previous two years.

I was sprung before first period. The full-bodied navy blue of the St Pat's uniform was an open invitation for the Leeds fluorescent yellow to beam all the more radiantly from my ankles. I pulled my trousers as low on the waist as they'd go, but the traffic lights were stuck on amber till sunset and there was no avoiding becoming the school's kid of the day. It was a mistake I wouldn't repeat. By the next morning it was all over, and no-one ever mentioned it again: there must have been some other poor sap on the conveyor belt to get stuck into.

The Leeds sock incident had been a blow to the ego, and I couldn't help but feel that cadets was a similar disaster in waiting. I could take all of the parading, the marching, the mind-numbing obtuseness of teaching boys to salute: it was the cadet camps, specifically the end-of-first-term expedition, that haunted me. A week-long bivouac (to add weight to the dread of the occasion, they seemed to have invented their own word for it) in the Grampians was the annual showpiece, seven days of things I'd be abysmal at – riding flying foxes; abseiling; hitching tents; cooking stale, army surplus beans – and it chilled me to the toenails every time I thought about it.

But I'd had an incredible stroke of luck. Early on in the piece I mentally pencilled in the date of the Year 9 endurance test: the first week of May. Miraculously, this coincided with the FA Cup final – the absolute unmissable TV event of the year, as Mum and Dad knew. It was the only alibi my parents might possibly let stick, and I reached a swift, perhaps slightly optimistic conclusion – *Sorry, Brother Atton*, making a silent pledge to the Christian Brother at the helm of the cadet corps, this was one pre-pubescent who wouldn't be parading in the wilds of the Wimmera that week.

Readers of February's new-look, two-man, junior-size *League Leader* knew Manchester United had already been eliminated from the Cup. Our results service reluctantly informed fans of the Red Devils of their 3–2 defeat by West Bromwich Albion in the fourth round, despite goals by Gordon Hill and n.a. ('not applicable' – we'd somehow decided it was a good way of saying we had no idea who'd scored the goal). N.a. had also tucked away a couple for the Gunners in the same period, reflecting the fact that, try as we might, and despite the technological wizardry of the late 1970s, we couldn't always get the information for which we hungered. The weekly soccer round-up in *The Age* was sketchy, and forking out $2 a minute to call the Arsenal or United switchboard – the only definitive source at our disposal – for the match-to-match minutiae wasn't an option. According to our financial projections, n.a. would be finding the net for a while to come.

In the wake of the United loss, Arsenal were putting together a decent FA Cup run. A 5–0 thrashing of second-division Sheffield United at their ground, our biggest away win for a decade, was followed by a last-minute defeat of Wolverhampton Wanderers and a 4–1 win against third-division Walsall. Fate seemed to be clearing a way through.

The Gunners were having a great season in the league, nestling in around fourth or fifth place. We were still a fair way from a serious championship challenge but, in the parallel world of the FA Cup, all you needed was for your luck to hold out for half-a-dozen games.

I'd be edgy before the announcement of the draw for each round: there was no seeding, so you might have to tackle a Liverpool or a Leeds at any time. It was slightly preposterous that we'd had such an easy run so far – we'd already been nominated as 1978's 'Their name's on the Cup' team – and when in the quarter-finals we were pitted against another third-division side, Wrexham, it seemed an open invitation from the football gods, or the Football Association at least, to dare to dream.

I was taking nothing for granted, though: in my three years supporting Arsenal I'd seen a few things. Even watching it on TV days after the game, the pinball parlour of scoring chances I had to sit through in the half-hour ABC match highlights had me shaking in my sensible shoes. And this despite the *Wrexham 2, Arsenal 3* result already recorded in my orange *1977–78* folder.

Almost before I'd registered, only the exotic – in name, anyway – Orient Football Club stood between Arsenal and our rightful place in the FA Cup final. Orient, who hailed from the east of London rather than the east of Earth, again resided in the nether lands of the league – nineteenth in the second division – and had been in the lower reaches for ninety-six of their 97-year existence. They'd never even made the FA Cup semi-finals before so, really, just winning their quarter-final against Middlesbrough must have been as good as actually lifting the Cup. So surely they wouldn't mind us sneaking past to claim the real thing …

Back in Australia, *League Leader,* without the steadying influence of a big-brother type, was getting a little avant-garde. In recent issues of the magazine, and with a nod to our Horsham roots, John and I had resurrected Andrew Smedley, Robert's soccer-loving

pig from Workington. In his latest incarnation, a self-
righteous Smedley played for a junior club, spending
most of the time falling over the ball and complaining
about his allegedly less skilful team mates. Funny stuff.

In John's absence, though, Mark grabbed Smedley
by the scruff of his ample neck. In *League Leader* issue
four, the jaunty headline above the cartoon – 'Football's
Fattest Footballer!' – was accurate enough, but, despite
opening with a semi-*vérité* drawing of Smedley hoofing
the ball deep into the stratosphere above Wembley
Stadium, the adventure ended, in a sub-Pink Floyd
post-hallucinogenic mist, with western Victoria's most
popular pig commandeering a Spitfire and preparing
for an aerial shoot-out with Baron Julius Horatius Von
Schnott. The tone arguably clashed a little with our
Four Corners-esque exposé of football hooliganism in
the UK and Methodist-sober wrap-up of the FA Cup
quarter-finals.

We'd filled a few pages with pigs in dogfights
and theses on thugs, but the major new recruit to
League Leader ranks, albeit without his consent as such,
was Uncle Shawn. John and I occasionally received
meticulously detailed letters from my uncle about
Arsenal, and precisely nothing else; just the way we
liked it. He'd write hieroglyphic five- or six-page match
reports, deconstructing games pass by pass in his
microscopic handwriting, full of words capitalised for
EMPHASIS, and brimming with ambitious theories

like: teams shouldn't buy players shorter than five foot eleven, and Spurs had scored at least one offside goal per home game since World War II. For some reason, it didn't occur to me to ask my uncle's permission to reprint his thoughts on our letters page.

However, Uncle Shawn didn't have it all his own way as he battled for space with some of the Ballarat soccer scene's finest minds. Seymour had infused his loathing of Liverpool into the consciousness of several of our readership, so their loss of a match on a weekend might be greeted by a letter from '3 United supporters', pointing out gleefully, though somewhat insanely, 'How come Liverpool had eleven players and a sub and could *still* complain of bad luck?'

Despite the stiff competition, my uncle – courtesy of paragraphs chosen from his letters, seemingly at random – quickly became our star correspondent. 'The Arsenal/Aston Villa game was the match when all our chickens came home to roost,' he wrote stridently, immediately concluding (thanks to our subtle cut-and-paste job), 'For one, if MacD was half the striker he used to be, we could have had several goals, and for another, Matthews did nothing to prove he's any better than Sunderland.' An angry Mr Mangan, Essex, England, was the signatory. The fact that most of our readers would have heard of neither (John) Matthews nor (Alan) Sunderland escaped our attention. Uncle Shawn began to single-handedly rule our letters page, without me ever bothering to mention it to him.

Before *League Leader* no. 4 had hit the shelves, I was on cloud no. 9. Arsenal had stormed past Orient 3–0 and we were in our first FA Cup final *ever* since I'd come on board. Now only fellow finalists Ipswich Town, struggling at the wrong end of the top division, stood between the Gunners and … and … well, you wouldn't want to jinx it by even thinking it too loud.

To the naked eye the victory against Orient had been regulation enough – they were a second-division team, after all. The match, though, featured a brilliant cameo by Supermac. Generally regarded as the greediest striker in the country, in the space of fifteen shameless minutes Macdonald hit two wayward, thunderbolt shots both destined for the corner flag before deflecting crazily into the net off an Orient defender. The sight of Supermac not only claiming both own goals as his own, but puffing his chest out like it had been parts 1 and 2 of a cunning plan, seemed, to some observers, to have an absurd, comic angle to it. For me, it just magnified the Macdonald legend.

Celia was breaking my heart. Someone had written a song about it. Dad was in Singapore to attend a medical conference and unfortunately he'd taken the missus with him. This left Anne and myself in the uncertain hands of a hormonally charged teenage family friend who had clearly let the power go to her head. Despite

my pleading, Celia Hogan had elected to send me out
on Ballarat's under-14 Kokoda Trail.

Mum and Dad had been around me for a while
now and understood where an Arsenal v Ipswich FA
Cup final might sit in the timeline of my personal
development. But in one of those little slips you might
chuckle about at their seventieth birthday party – and
not much earlier – they hadn't communicated the gravity
of the situation to Celia, and she mistakenly assumed
the role of normal, responsible parent. Incredibly,
she felt that a week with my peers testing the very
essence of myself as the first taste of winter lashed
the Grampians mattered more than some Pommy
soccer team booting a ball around against some other
Pommy soccer team. At Wembley Stadium. In front
of a worldwide audience numbering several hundred
million. In the match of my life.

I lay in an army-issue bed at the cadet camp,
wondering if I was as ill as I'd decided I wanted to
be. Looking out the flap of the drab khaki tent, with
100 teenagers in camouflage whirring past outside, the
clop of army boots battling with the humming engines
of school buses departing the mountains for Ballarat,
I choked on the disappointment and frustration. I'd
been thinking along these lines: Arsenal might never
reach an FA Cup final again.

It wasn't such a ridiculous idea. Liverpool, Chelsea
and Leeds, for instance, only had four FA Cup wins

between them in 300 years of collective existence. Given Arsenal's previous strike rate of zero Cup final appearances in the years I'd supported the team – an unpromising 0 per cent – it would have been rash to assume the game against Ipswich wouldn't be my sole opportunity to see the Gunners in the spotlight. And where was I at their moment of glory? At the foot of a mountain range on the other side of the planet, my baggy Australian army uniform hanging loosely on a body racked with regret.

Nonetheless, once I'd accepted that lying in bed for a week, sidelined solely by bitterness, wasn't an option, I ventured out into the rocky fray. It was a bivouac, alright, with marching, saluting, fire-lighting, tent-erecting and eating Anzac biscuits made of brick the order of the day. Actually, in retrospect it kind of sounds like fun.

At the time, I hated the lot of it. The first day dragged by, then the second; then it was the day of the Cup final. The match was played at midnight on the Saturday, and I laboured through Sunday, knowing the FA Cup had been won and lost without me, with millions of fans from Ballarat to Buenos Aires digesting the result hours after the issue had been settled.

It was flying-fox day too. You grabbed onto a rope suspended in mid-air several hundred feet – okay, maybe several hundred inches – above the ground and careered down a cable from one side of a hypothetical

gorge to another. Some volunteered, some were pushed
– these were tense times.

Eventually, the sun set and we were closing in on
6.02 p.m.: high noon. I snuck away from the camp fire
as a couple of cadets in my platoon set some cans of
year-old baked beans among the embers. Burrowing
into the tent, I lay on my grubby sleeping bag, searching
in the dark for 3WV. The reception wasn't bad, and
the six o'clock news headlines passed in slow motion
before the BBC World Service sports round-up.

The FA Cup would be the lead story of the day,
so I knew the first handful of words would be decisive.
The opening theme of the program faded into a wall
of ecstatic crowd noise that seemed to last for minutes.
Then the unnervingly even tone of a well-trained voice
enunciated the phrase, 'Mick Mills …'

They were two words that might pass unnoticed on
most days in most walks of life. On 6 May 1978, though,
the name of the Ipswich captain, drowned in cheering,
could mean only one thing – Arsenal had lost the Cup.
Almost catatonic, I listened to the match report staring
through the dark at the sagging roof of the tent. The
Gunners, unexpectedly injury-ridden, had been beaten
by a goal after seventy-seven minutes by Ipswich's
journeyman, nobody, no-hoper Roger Osborne, who'd
had to be substituted seconds later, due to 'a touch of
sunstroke and emotion'. Malcolm Macdonald hadn't
been sighted, and we'd been outplayed by a team about

to finish thirteen places below us in the league. It was pure humiliation.

I could hear laughter outside, and it smelled like the beans were done. But what did I care about food? Ipswich 1, Arsenal 0. FA Cup losers. I looked into the blackness, feeling let down by everyone I could think of, from Celia to Supermac. And it wasn't as if the good times were just around the corner: in a few hours the reveille bugle would be sounding again and who knew what remorseless tests of physical endurance might lie in wait? I stepped out of the tent and headed for the fire, the words 'Mick' and 'Mills' digging a pit in my stomach, wondering if this might be the worst day of my life.

Impending Depression

The Ballarat soccer season couldn't come soon enough. The closest I'd been to a competitive match in the previous eight months was a sticky 35°C January day when John – a couple of weeks before his boarding-school defection – Seymour and I donned our Manchester United, Arsenal and England kits and carted ourselves over to the open spaces of Mark's home ground, the Welcome Stranger caravan park, for a photo shoot.

It was a simple, but baffling idea. For starters, we stage-managed John posing as an agonisingly stretched-out goalkeeper, while Seymour, equally frozen, strained every available tendon to hammer an invisible ball past him into the notional net. They stood, epically statuesque, Mark's right leg hovering in mid-air for minutes at a time while I, as photographer, pondered how best to capture the energy of the moment.

Then we swapped and Seymour choreographed a heading duel between me and John. We could do this for hours and call it entertainment, with the Welcome

Stranger as good as mutating into Wembley – swings in the background flaking green paint, corrugated-iron fences creaking in an aching northerly wind and a preponderance of Franklin 3-bed pop tops notwithstanding. What out-of-town park visitors made of our football Tai Chi is anyone's guess; but it couldn't have been good for tourism.

With winter nearing, and the memory fading of our still-life soccer, I was ready for the real thing. The onset of the 1978 Ballarat campaign offered me the chance of redemption, to break my goal-scoring duck at last. Granted, as a winger, finding the onion bag wasn't the focus, but a whole first season and not one goal had to hurt my Socceroo prospects. It had been almost three years since my solitary strike in an actual game, back in primary school, back in pre-history against Ararat.

St Pat's under-14s' season opener was against Ballarat College. It was a tricky assignment, the College junior XI a complete mystery despite the school being only a side street away. We fancied our chances, though, with the likes of Seymour and Dominic Barba – still buzzing from his *Red 'n' White* poster-competition triumph the previous year – in our ranks: my chronic goallessness mightn't matter.

The match proved to be a typical high-octane derby, but we'd just about shaded it when, with fifteen minutes left, the ball broke loose inside the penalty area. I knew the time had come. I remember the chaos of the battlefield, bodies flinging themselves between me and the goal, then a Zen-like calm descending on the Shed Oval. As the ball fell to my favoured left foot, I took a touch to control it and, before my mind could register the fear, I'd belted it into the net. Yaaahh! I went berserk – by my standards, anyway. Clenching my fist, giving a minimal shriek that bared three or four teeth, I ran in an ecstatic haze back to the halfway line.

Seymour, though as well-versed as the rest of us in the adolescent male art of grudging praise, couldn't help himself: he knew how much the goal meant to me. 'Good one, Arsenal,' he smiled cheesily. The rest of the team, perhaps not recognising the crippling weight lifted from my shoulders with my first ever strike in the big city, were more nonchalant. Dominic Barba gave me the kind of nod you might get in the corridors at lunchtime. His indifference was understandable: we were winning 14–0 and he'd scored eleven.

To everyone's amazement I got another goal later in the match and tucked away my third in two games at Ballarat High the following week. Next, it was Ballarat College again – at least that's who they said they were – though they were unrecognisable, conjuring a 16-goal turnaround in a tough 3–3 draw. After the game I wrote a two-page report of how the season was shaping up, with a no-holds-barred analysis of the second match against College. I didn't spare myself: 'stifled by the College defence'; 'only an average game', I said of me. Dissecting our fixtures player by player, with team line-ups and progressive scorers for the season – then painstakingly typing it all up in a newsletter format – was fairly obsessive even by my standards. Perhaps I was in denial, trying to keep myself occupied as life off the field turned against me.

With John in Melbourne and the Gunners having blown their best FA Cup opportunity maybe for decades, I was dreading the phone call that was eventually patched through: Mark had been summoned to England. His mum and Jason had found a place near Norwich, he told me excitedly one morning recess, and he'd be leaving for the UK in a couple of weeks. Having survived a dispiriting few months stranded in a dormitory at St Pat's, Seymour was elated, anticipating an epic adventure far from the Christian brothers. This was alright for him, but I have to say it didn't do much for me.

While Seymour imagined the glamour of the far east of England – Clacton on Sea and Walton on the Naze just had to be something special – there was some housekeeping to complete: the final edition of *League Leader*. Volume one, number six seemed to mirror the times. The magazine distractedly contained both a preview of the forthcoming World Cup finals and a match report of Argentina's subsequent victory, while the editorial claimed the thirty-cent cost for the double issue was excellent value, contradicting the figure on the cover: fifteen cents. Topping things off, the Smedley cartoon ended with a forgetful 'To Be Continued'.

On the upside, we'd scooped an interview with Alun Evans. Yes, *the* Alun Evans. He'd been a star with Liverpool in the early 1970s, scoring the BBC Goal of the Year in 1971, but a nightclub incident in which he'd been scarred by broken glass signalled a downturn in his fortunes that led – *very* gradually – to the blue and white of South Melbourne.

Inevitably, within minutes of Evans unpacking his suitcases at Middle Park, I wrote to him. Much less inevitably he wrote straight back, answering very pleasantly my harmless, meticulously handwritten page of questions. There was one answer that shocked me: the best coach he'd had, he said, was Liverpool's Bill Shankly – 'bye a mile'. I looked at the letter half-a-dozen times, hardly comprehending that someone capable of scoring a hat-trick against Bayern Munich – UEFA Cup quarter-final, March 1971 – might be a little iffy with his spelling. Nonetheless, Alun was our most famous interviewee ever by the length of Sturt Street and, without so much as a bye your leave, I plonked his private correspondence onto pages ten and eleven.

Stoics that we were, the farewell issue wasn't about to sink into hopeless nostalgia. However our fearlessly opinionated columnist Mark Seymour didn't let our demise pass without comment. 'Just you remember that there's only two of us running this thing,' he wrote, with perhaps a trifle more indignation than was required. 'We struggle and work our guts out,' he continued angrily, asserting that it had been arduous enough for me and him, 'let alone leaving the burden on one pair of tiny shoulders', as he accurately put it.

Seymour had barely signed off on his agitated editorial before he was leaving on a Qantas flight for Norwich. While Brother Zoch farewelled him with prayers and speeches, Mark's and my goodbye was more informal. We promised to stay in touch: Seymour providing updates from the nerve centre of the real world; me reminding him of how pleased he was to have left western Victoria behind.

Spring was dawning in Australia, a time of hope, expectation and the relentless singing of birds. Mark would arrive in England at the tail end of their week and a half of summer, to a country bracing itself for six long months of cold fronts and depressions: in other words, he'd be there at the start of the soccer season. He couldn't believe his luck. Everything was coming up roses, for one of us at least. I was happy for him – just.

J.U.S.T.I.C.E.

Mr Farley, our long-serving Latin teacher, cut a pretty compelling figure. A stout man with a bawdy sense of humour and, appropriately, a volcanic Latin temper despite his Anglo bloodline, he'd recite *Tarquinius Superbus, septimus rex Romanorum, durus et scelestus homo erat* like his life was at stake. No matter how superbus Tarquinius was, though, it was a hard sell to distracted fourteen-year-olds, and it was amazing he succeeded in imbuing us with even a vague interest in the subject. I found languages kind of interesting myself, but after Seymour's departure you could say I'd lost a little *joie de vivre*. At the end of the hour, with the second and third declension nouns struggling to sink in, I'd dawdle out of class into the eucalypt-dappled sunshine, not quite knowing what to do with myself.

The onset of the English football season might have cheered me up, if it hadn't been for Mick Mills. The FA Cup final still came to me in dreams – I hadn't clapped eyes on Roger Osborne's winning goal against us yet, but it was as vivid as if I'd been one of his boots.

Nevertheless, Arsenal hadn't had a bad season: it was a far cry from the back-to-back relegation years. And, incredibly, we'd be joined for the 1978/79 campaign by an Australian, Socceroo striker John Kosmina having joined the club in a low-budget £15,000 move from West Adelaide – although he'd immediately disappeared into the Arsenal reserves.

Despite the dull, lingering pain, I listened to the BBC sports round-up on the first Sunday evening of the season on our way home from Mass. Arsenal had drawn 2–2 at home to Leeds – not great, but not bad – and from the front of the Renault the announcer coolly observed that the Gunners had finished with seven Irishmen, a Scotsman and an Australian on the field.

I gawped at the radio, reflecting on the ramifications. As far as I knew only two Aussies had ever played in the English first division, so this was something. I'd watched Kosmina in the Philips Soccer League on the 0/10 Network, and now he was wearing an Arsenal shirt, sharing the turf with Supermac, Pat Jennings, David O'Leary, Frank Stapleton, Graham Rix, and all the other names that rolled off the tongue like a home phone number.

It was a pivotal moment. There was an Aussie playing for the Gunners: one of *us* playing for *us*. I'd started off barracking for the Gunners as a link with the past – family, nationality and all that – and it didn't quite click that Arsenal had taken on a life of its own as a kind of sovereign state, almost completely removed from its British origins. My Englishness might have been diluted over the years, but I'd only become more of an Arsenal fan, and more of an Australian, during the same period. To summarise, it seemed like Kossie was one of us who'd made the big time over there (at home) – well, I couldn't quite work it out either.

Regrettably, the Leeds fixture wasn't the launching pad for a stellar Highbury career for Kosmina, who played only three more matches for the first team. A few months later he was back in Australia, treading the boards again for West Adelaide – having to content himself with eventually winning 100 caps for the Socceroos, in the process becoming the top scorer in the history of the national team. Scant consolation, obviously. So maybe he'd failed to make an impact in the English first division, but the four Arsenal games under his belt forever gold-plated the man in my eyes.

While the Kossie worship had been a welcome diversion, life was still a poor imitation of its former self. School was a drudge without Mark's courageously opinionated analysis of his morning classes, and with the demise of *League Leader* I didn't even have a day job to distract me. But to my credit I wasn't entirely frittering my time away on log tables and *To Kill a Mockingbird*. Like someone who'd lost his leg but could still feel it there somewhere, I was determined to press on with the Ballarat soccer publishing machine.

My latest, somewhat desperate project was – okay, unfathomably – to make a match-day program for my favourite Australian national league club, Fitzroy United Alexander, in its forthcoming clash with the Yugoslav-supported Footscray JUST.

Admittedly it wouldn't have been my chosen category on *Mastermind*, but, thanks to my folder spilling over with riveting statistics from the English and Australian leagues, I had a PhD's worth of Philips Soccer League information at my disposal. I was deep into pre-production before I realised the match was at Footscray's home ground not Fitzroy's, and therefore, for the purposes of rigorous authenticity, the program would have to be written from a JUST perspective. Thus, upbeat – but a little half-hearted – articles about, say, Footscray's declining attendances ('Our crowds down – but only by 333'), were peppered throughout the magazine.

Elsewhere I foresaw, with unerring precision, that 15,627 fans would flock to that weekend's Adelaide City v West Adelaide encounter, while I was equally convinced table-topping Marconi would take the points against Newcastle: 'Marconi to Increase Lead Again', I wrote with a firm hand. Changing my mind after a vision received on deadline, however, I was fooling no-one with the amateurishly, blue-pen doctored: 'Marconi to Decrease Lead Again'. To make matters worse, only 13,051 turned up for the Adelaide fixture.

Unperturbed I decided, cajoled by John, calling in weekly from the payphone in the Great Hall at Xavier, to send the program to the actual Footscray JUST. For legal protection, I stamped the word 'Unofficial' on the top left-hand corner of the cover – in case anyone at Footscray wouldn't notice the text was entirely in biro, or that the front-page photo was secured by Blu-Tack – mailed it to their Schintler Reserve headquarters in Melbourne's light-industrial west, and more or less forgot all about it.

Weeks later I was staggered to receive a package from a JUST official, Lou Tonovski, containing not only my program – now adorned with a sprawl of Footscray autographs – but an invitation to be the club's guest and meet the players at JUST's next match. I hadn't had much of a year, but this was brilliant. *Footscray JUST against Fitzroy Alexander at Olympic Park, possible attendance 6500*, I told myself, a little dazed, the quantum leap to first personal contact with the real adult soccer world standing before me.

I could never have carried this off solo – Mum wouldn't let me, anyway – so I got John on board. He'd been in Melbourne for a few months now and, meeting me at Spencer Street station, conveyed a casual air of boarding-school, big-city know-how. He knew that conductors on orange trams had their own little ticket booth, while green-tram conductors walked around with satchels; he knew which queue to get into outside

Olympic Park; he could spell 'souvlaki'.

It's difficult to express what being in the vicinity of Footscray JUST meant to me. Courtesy of the *Philips Top Soccer* show every Saturday night on the 0/10 Network (I fully endorsed their claim to be 'Turning it on for the Good Times'), the likes of Zdravko Lujic, Joe Picioane and Igor Hazabent were bona fide celebrities. Igor and co. had faced Supermac, Charlie George, John Kosmina etc in the PSL on a week-to-week basis, while a couple of the Footscray team had been professionals in Europe, brushing shin pads with former team mates of footballers who might once have played against – or perhaps known someone who'd played against – maybe Pele or George Best. There was a direct line to greatness here, and no matter how famous a Dennis Lillee or Olympic sprinter Raelene Boyle might be within their limited field, they didn't, ultimately, have anything on the glamour of JUST.

Beyond the turnstiles at the stadium, we made our way to the Footscray dressing room, fending off clouds of Slavic and Mediterranean cigarette smoke and, after a tussle with a reluctant doorman, we were in. Lou Tonovski, a bubbly, youngish bloke, greeted us, escorting John and me down a stark, echoing corridor towards the inner sanctum of the Philips Soccer League. Once through the gateway, the scene in the dressing room was psychedelic. Within the white, prison-like walls there was the odour of liniment floating across the room, sheets of chest hair, exotic, secret-agent accents, the clack of boot studs on concrete, with someone flinging a notebook about while a photographer snapped madly away. It was a gluttonous assault on the senses, and roughly half of it was the fault of Jim Kriaris.

Kriaris, JUST's middle-aged defender, was retiring after the game and the notebook-wielding Laurie Schwab, soccer writer for *The Age* and editor of *Soccer Action* magazine, plus photographer, were there to crystallise the moment. Mr Tonovski sidestepped the two-man media throng and took us around the room, introducing us to the Footscray team. Most of them remembered my blue-biro match program and seemed overjoyed to meet a club supporter all the way from Ballarat. (In my defence, I was becoming more of a JUST fan by the minute.) Even Jim Kriaris, his footballing life probably flashing before his eyes, gave me a manly grin.

A close encounter of the third kind with the Footscray JUST squad was reason enough to register a red-letter day, but meeting Laurie Schwab was as much of a thrill. I'd seen his photo in eighty or ninety issues of *Soccer Action*, with that characteristic full beard you could almost swim in (if you were inclined to), and he was at least as intimidating as the towel-clad man-mountains surrounding him. To my amazement, Laurie seemed vaguely interested in us and the match program, asking me a swag of questions (in a fit of magnanimity, or maybe pre-match nerves, I told him Mark was co-author) before getting back to work. It seemed absurd, but I'd just been interviewed by Australia's most influential soccer magazine.

The game itself was almost an afterthought. Despite my dressing-room reception fit for a Yugoslav pop star, I still had a hankering for Fitzroy Alexander to win the match. They didn't, but watching Kriaris applauded off the ground by 4000 supporters after the match, sweat plastering his lank hair to his forehead as he loped across Olympic Park's running track for the last time, JUST's 1–0 victory seemed a reasonable outcome.

The following Wednesday I spent a distracted hour and a half in the Regent Theatre watching *Grease*, claiming to be there under protest escorting my sister, but I had to admit a certain fascination with Olivia Neutron-Bomb. Under normal circumstances Rydell High's all-dancing passion play would have diminished, or at least refocused, my troubles. But on a regular day Arsenal wouldn't have been playing ramshackle third-division Rotherham United in a ticklish League Cup tie.

It was the type of game, early season and Supermac and friends still rusty, in which an underdog might spring a nasty surprise. I was entering season four without a trophy under my belt and, while the League

Cup came a distant, barely visible third behind the
league championship and FA Cup in the fans' pecking
order, it looked pretty good to me. The previous
season, in the corresponding match, John and I had
been there in the boys' enclosure for the League Cup
defeat of Manchester United. A loss that evening would
have been a blow, but succumbing to Rotherham was
unthinkable. Their nickname was the Merry Millers, for
crying out loud.

It was 4 p.m. and the first edition of *The Herald*
would be in Ballarat by now. I left Anne outside the
Regent in the hands of a couple of her irresponsible
friends and raced down Lydiard Street to the newsagent.
Third page from the back, the broadsheet pages too big
for my fingers to come to grips with quickly enough,
there it was: racing results, golf, dogs, basketball, rugby,
but the words *League Cup* were like a neon light.

> English soccer, League Cup, Second Round:
> Bolton Wanderers 2 Chelsea 1 Brighton and
> Hove Albion 1 Millwall 0 Burnley 1 Bradford
> City 1 Everton 8 Wimbledon 0 Preston North
> End 1 Queens Park Rangers 3 Rotherham
> United 3 Arsenal 1 Swansea City 2 Tottenham
> Hotspur 2 Wrexham 1 Norwich City 3.

I traced my finger along the drunken string of scores
a couple of times before confirming the worst.

Rotherham. Losing to Ipswich in the Grampians had been sickening, but at least there'd been some dignity there. But a 3–1 defeat by Rotherham – it wasn't even a fluky 1–0 – was nearly unforgivable. Back in England, Gunners fans were waking on a dismal morning, their Arsenal-loathing friends and relations enjoying the eight or nine hours' rest to hone their taunts. *Bloody Rotherham? They couldn't beat a flippin' egg.* The Gunners were 300 games and counting since our last trophy.

With the Merry Millers on my mind, I almost didn't notice that in my mid-week reflex, I'd bought the latest *Soccer Action*. In the wake of the League Cup defeat the fortunes of JUST, Alexander and the rest would struggle to compete, but I thumbed dutifully through the first few pages. Glancing nostalgically at the JUST match report – I'd *been* at that game – there was a photo of Jim Kriaris accepting an engraved salver from the pork-pie-hatted Footscray president. To the right was an article, 'Kriaris To Coach', and below a smaller headline, 'Staunch fans'. Only half paying attention I saw my own name stamped in black and white on the page. And John's. And Mark's.

> Patrick Mangan, 14, made the 100-km journey from Ballarat to watch Footscray J.U.S.T. at Olympic Park and to meet the players. Patrick's older brother John, 15, who goes to boarding school in Melbourne, came along.

Patrick had with him a booklet on J.U.S.T. and the Philips League. He and a friend, Mark Seymour, had compiled it. In the J.U.S.T. rooms before the match, the players signed autographs for the boys and wished them well.

League Cup? What League Cup? There wasn't much that could have shunted Arsenal's worst defeat in years off my emotional front page, but seeing my name up in lights seemed to do the trick. In two-and-a-half years of *Soccer Action* they'd never identified anyone as *staunch*: I'd been earmarked as one of the nation's premier soccer supporters. This was recognition on an inconceivable level, and I almost fainted with sheer body-bursting excitement.

Skipping back up Lydiard Street to the Regent, my heart ricocheting off my ribs, I tried to get my head around what I'd achieved. Anne was in the exact spot I'd left her, when the world had been a slightly different, less welcoming place. She was locked in a round of fevered *Grease* post-mortems, but I nearly abandoned my big-brother cool and giddily revealed to her and her uninterested friends the two paragraphs on page seven that had made my year.

In bed that night still buzzing with the glory of it all, the Rotherham incident an occasional unfortunate diversion, I contemplated the paradox here. Okay, with my brother and Mark miles if not continents away, I was as lonely as I'd been in my life. On the other hand I was now an Australian soccer celebrity. There was something else peculiar – Arsenal had had a horrendous day and I'd had a great one. Call me slow, but the fact that my life could move forward independently of the Gunners had never occurred to me. *They could lose and I could still win.* As epiphanies go it was pretty lame – but there you are.

Part V

Part V

Iran So Far Away

1977, 1981, 1985, 1989, 1993. If you say it quickly, it almost doesn't sound like that long a time. What it represented, though, was inescapable – twenty-three years of World Cup failure.

It had begun back in August 1977. Within a week of Enfield's part-timers putting the Kuwait national team to the sword, the Socceroos played a qualification match against Iran in Melbourne and lost 1–0 after missing a penalty. Two months after that, they were well beaten at the Sydney Sports Ground by – *of course* – Kuwait, and were effectively out of the next year's World Cup finals. Watching that game on the ABC, it was ridiculous to think that the mesmeric Kuwaitis were the same team that had trundled through their match against the 'E's.

Four years later and the next campaign: the good news was that Aussie striker Gary Cole now featured in the *Guinness Book of Records* for the most goals ever scored in a World Cup match, bagging seven in a 10–0 win against Fiji. The bad news was that the Socceroos were all but out of contention for a finals place by then. New Zealand stole a 3–3 draw with Australia in Auckland, coming back from a goal down on three occasions, before beating us 2–0 at the Sydney Cricket Ground; and that was pretty much that.

Happy to leap onto any bandwagon this side of Guam, I wrote to the Kiwi forward Steve Wooddin, the envelope resplendent with my school crest because I couldn't find any others. It probably wasn't the most exciting letter he received in 1981 – maybe not even that day – but, brilliantly, he wrote back, gamely tackling pedestrian questions such as 'Who were Australia's best players when you played against them?' with replies like 'In the 2 games we played them, hardly any of them were any good. We know they are all good players and am quite happy with the way they all played against NZ'. When Steve took to the field in the World Cup finals in Spain against Scotland, Russia and Brazil, I felt he'd taken a little piece of me onto the park with him. Arguably quite a dull piece.

In 1985, the problems really began to take root, and it was all Socceroos coach Frank Arok's fault. He instilled such confidence in his team and its supporters that we began to imagine we actually had a snowball's chance of World Cup qualification. At the time, the Australians weren't taken seriously enough to be granted fixtures against most half-decent international teams, so the outspoken Arok had to content himself with leading his self-styled 'mad dogs' to occasionally bruising wins against the likes of Juventus, Spurs, Rangers and Red Star Belgrade. And in the early World Cup games, the Socceroos swept aside Israel and New Zealand and found themselves just one hurdle away from their first World Cup appearance in a dozen years. That hurdle, though, was Scotland.

Before the first match in Glasgow, the ever-quotable Arok said unnecessarily, 'We are not a bunch of cuddly koalas,' and noted that the Scottish team – among them Kenny Dalglish and Graeme Souness, two of the best players in Europe – weren't infallible. The Scots only had two legs, he said, adding deadpan, 'Some of them even have heads.'

John was in the UK at the time and bought a ticket from a scalper for the sell-out match at Hampden Park. With not a single Australian flag, shirt or scarf visible in the 60,000 crowd – about half of whom seemed to be wearing the unlikely ensemble of kilt and runners – he decided to play it low key when Scotland scored against the obdurate Aussies. Although the locals appeared at least as interested in chanting anti-English slogans as cheering their own team, the goal had the expected effect and John was half-smothered by a swarm of delirious Scots hugging everyone within arm's reach and slightly beyond. The 2–0 final result all but guaranteed the Tartan Army a place in the finals, although John and I hadn't quite abandoned hope.

The return match was at Melbourne's Olympic
Park on a bowling-green pitch on a pleasant early
summer's evening. It sounds delightful, but Arok
was livid. He hadn't been joking when he'd suggested
playing the classy Scotland team in the midday heat in
a dust bowl in Orange. Orange was harder to get to by
tram, though, so I wasn't entirely against the Australian
Soccer Federation's decision, and I squeezed in among
29,500 fans at a stadium more used to crowds a tenth
of the size.

Although I was at the ground, I remember the match
more by the TV coverage – the Welsh TV coverage,
strangely enough. Uncle Kevin – one of the uncles in
the smoke-hazy living room at my grandparents' place
in London back in 1973 – lived in Wales and taped
the match, mailing us the video soon after. And for all
the bravado of the pre-match coverage down under
– the Melbourne *Herald* featured an upbeat four-page
'Winfield Socceroos' wraparound – watching the tape
months later, I had to admit that the Welsh television
analysis was probably more realistic.

George Best was a guest on the Welsh morning
show and was asked by the Argyle-sweatered host,
'Can you see any way at all that Australia can cause big
problems for Scotland?' 'To be quite honest, I don't,'
replied George, not trying too hard to be diplomatic.
'I was over in Australia recently and the standard isn't
that good.'

In the event, the Socceroos played like demons, and as a couple of million Scots almost choked on their breakfast, only a succession of great saves and near misses kept the score line blank. 'The gods are smiling undoubtedly on the Scotsmen,' commentator Jock Brown's voice dripped with relief as another scoring chance was spurned by the home team. It ended 0–0 and Australia was out.

None of us were getting any younger and, as far as the Socceroos were concerned, I was beginning to think I'd seen it all. The 1989 campaign appeared to bear that out, as a familiar 2–0 defeat against New Zealand – in a match bizarrely played as a lunchtime curtain-raiser for a provincial rugby fixture – pushed Australia to the brink of elimination. Needing a win against Israel at the newly unveiled Sydney Football Stadium, a controversial 1–1 draw sealed our fate.

By 1993, I was facing my fifth tour of duty and anything but failure seemed unthinkable. Nonetheless, I flew to Sydney and saw us defeat Canada – the untried, surfie-haired goalkeeper Mark Schwarzer saving two penalties in a miraculous, once-in-a-lifetime display. Our reward was a playoff, not against teams we probably couldn't beat, like New Zealand, but the two-time world champions Argentina.

I was on the plane to the harbour city again – John too – for the unmissable opportunity to see Diego Maradona in the flesh. It was surreal, like having an audience with Humphrey Bogart, or Moses, someone you knew didn't belong in your Australian suburban world. But there he was, the day after his thirty-third birthday, gliding across the turf, partially obscured from view for the entire ninety minutes by his Melburnian shadow, the almost legendary Paul Wade. When the Argentine ace picked up the ball to take a throw-in on our side of the field, 5000 people leaned onto the edge of their seats, trying to suck in some Maradona oxygen. Dizzying though Diego's presence was, I was still desperate to see his team hammered; I guess that was never going to happen, but a 1–1 draw was honourable, to say the least.

In the return match in Argentina, on a chopped-up pitch littered with ticker tape, the Socceroos withstood an onslaught – mainly from the crowd. All 60,000 locals jumped up and down simultaneously as the River Plate Stadium swayed and shook. Awestruck Aussie midfielder Robbie Slater tried to describe the atmosphere in his autobiography *The Hard Way*: 'The people became the stadium. The stadium became the people. It was frightening.'

Despite the daunting backdrop, Australia had the ball in the net twice – both times ruled out for offside – and Adelaide City forward Carl Veart skewed the ball wide in the ninety-first minute. Argentina deservedly prevailed, though, 1–0, albeit with an outlandish goal. Fifty-eight minutes in, Gabriel Batistuta tried to drive in a right-footed cross from the edge of the penalty area, the ball struck Socceroos defender Alex Tobin – 'the 27-year-old draughtsman', commentator Andy Paschalidis lucidly spelling out the difference between the two teams – then looped crazily skyward and somehow ended up in the net.

'Australia always seem to go out to that type of goal,' said a crestfallen Johnny Warren afterwards, although his audience might have been slightly distracted by the peculiar angle attained by his hair in the stiff Buenos Aires breeze. The famous Warren locks may have been agitated on the day, but the natural order of things had been otherwise maintained: the Socceroos were where they belonged, on the sidelines looking on ruefully.

In November 1997, as I walked into the media conference area after the match against Iran, I wasn't conscious of the couple of decades of Australian soccer failure underpinning the events of the previous forty-five minutes. I wasn't contemplating the devious Kuwaitis, the man of letters Steve Wooddin, the panicking Scots, or the ball somehow completing its eccentric arc nestled in the Australian net in Buenos Aires.

Amid the clatter of cameras being erected at the back of the room, microphones splayed across the front table, virtually no-one said a word. The overwhelming mood among us was bewilderment, like we'd just woken up and weren't quite sure where we were. Reliving the memory of Australia being 2–0 ahead and in cruise control, a roomful of people seemed to be wondering, 'How the hell did *that* happen?'

All I could compute was the bizarreness of it. The Socceroos had hammered one of the best teams in Asia, creating a trail of almost unmissable chances; it could easily have been 7–0 or 8–0. But all that was forgotten beneath a headline that made a mockery of what we'd witnessed. In short: 'Australia Blows It'.

It had been the opposite of the sedate second half I'd required to complete my match report in peace. In the fiftieth minute, with the Socceroos leading 2–0, a fellow named Peter Hore had run onto the field and determinedly, inexplicably, torn down the net. The game was stopped for six minutes. The net-effect: the demoralised Iranians had a chance to regroup. Quite pleased with the extra time to hone my victorious opening paragraphs, I was still juggling a few flamboyant adjectives as Karim Bagheri, in maybe Iran's second attack of the game, poked the ball past Mark Bosnich after some muddled defending: 2–1.

At some stage in the previous twenty minutes, in the TV gantry not far from us, SBS commentator Johnny Warren had no doubt uttered one of his favourite truisms: that 2–0 is a dangerous lead. It breeds complacency, he liked to say. The Socceroos didn't need reminding – now.

As Bagheri's shot rippled the net, the Australian team – from the boyish Harry Kewell and jet-booted Stan Lazaridis to the veterans of Argentina '93 Robbie Slater and draughtsman Alex Tobin – remembered that this was a World Cup elimination match. That it wasn't the training exercise it had felt like for seventy-five minutes. That it was two goals to one now, not the 6–0 it should have been. That if Iran scored again, Australia was out. And that the Socceroos were notoriously, inevitably unlucky when it counted most.

Three minutes later, the game was up. After a towering header by Ali Daei, the disastrously skilful Khodadad Azizi scurried through the Socceroos' haphazard offside trap and coolly slotted in the equaliser. He leaped over a pitch-side hoarding and hurtled towards a parade of expatriate Iranian flags as a resigned hush descended on the rest of the MCG. We all seemed to realise, instantly, that there wasn't a hope in a million the Australians would recover from here. We were right. Eight minutes of injury time was nowhere near enough: 2–2. Iran had won on away goals. The Socceroos were out.

It was a typical evening in the press box, a silently frenetic roomful of journalists attending to ruined match reports. Everyone was honing their opening line: *We're out of the World Cup for another four years.* It was catastrophic, but it wasn't my problem – not yet, anyway. I was a bit distracted by deadlines; only a few minutes to submit my piece and I hardly knew where to begin.

One of the sub-editors – my beer-supplying friend Mick – rang almost immediately. He needed to know just one detail: how long before the end did Iran score their goals? It was a fair question, and in every other match I'd ever seen the answer would have been as plain as the shiny green shirt on my back. Bagheri seventy-sixth minute; Azizi seventy-ninth. But in all the confusion I couldn't be sure the clock wasn't stopped for the six-minute net repairs, so the Socceroos had been eleven, or possibly seventeen, minutes from World Cup qualification when Iran had equalised. It would have been good to know which.

We settled on eleven and I hit 'send'. As my match report was ejected into space, I nearly keeled over with relief. I'd done it. Five hundred words. And I was nearly half convinced I hadn't written anything quotably bad or irredeemably stupid – with the possible exception of the six-minute thing. On Sunday morning, tens of thousands of Victorians would flick past the page detailing one of the ugliest results in Australian soccer history – but at least it wouldn't be blank.

Pulsing with adrenaline, so much that the disappointment hadn't yet got me in the stomach, I crossed the serenely floodlit turf to where the media conference was taking place. There was a cluster of spectators left in the stands, sporting Socceroo shirts as garish as mine and boxing kangaroo flags hanging limp, seemingly determined not to leave the stadium; that if they stuck around long enough a replay might be announced, on the unprecedented grounds of Travesty of Justice.

The media conference was a peculiar postscript. With forty or fifty journalists looking on, the Iran coach Valdeir Vieira was almost contrite. 'God has helped us, we were lucky,' he said quietly. 'They played ten times better than we did.' Socceroos coach Terry Venables, sitting next to him, felt he had to reach over and gee Vieira up. 'You did very well,' he smiled weakly, possibly imagining he'd be a little more upbeat if *he'd* just become a national hero to sixty million Iranians. Venables croakily added later, 'I feel really, really low,' maybe contemplating whether – just on the off-chance – he was a hero himself for guiding Australia to its fourteenth straight match without defeat, or if, having been paid a fortune and failed, he ought to hitch a ride on the next stage out of town.

An hour later, after submitting a few paragraphs about the media conference for the late, late edition of the paper, I was out of there myself in a taxi heading home. It was weird being outside the MCG again beyond the universe of the Socceroos v Iran, the battle for the last spot at France '98, the invisible presence of hundreds of millions of Asian and European TV viewers, Australia being the focal point of the world game – anywhere on the planet – for a fairly dramatic hour and a half. I'd nearly forgotten the city of Melbourne was outside, where a frail-looking person in a bottle-green beacon of a shirt might be thought odd. 'You been at the soccer?' the taxi driver astutely asked.

It was a tactical error, and I assailed the poor bloke – we had *five* clear-cut chances in the first ten minutes; *five* – for the length of the journey. To his credit he appeared to be trying to keep up, but he looked happy enough to grab the fare and say his goodbyes as he dropped me off at the plasterboard bungalow. I turned on the lights and glanced at the alarm clock on the muggy, swirly-brown carpet beside the floor-level mattress. Midnight.

It had been a nothing day, really. The Socceroos had begun the evening not in the World Cup finals and ended it in the same place. I'd written another match report for *The Sunday Age* that no-one much would be inclined to read. And twenty-four hours earlier soccer had been the sleeping giant of Australian sport and, unremarkably, it still was. You had to admit it was funny, though, that the Australian team had all but won, that they'd actually drawn, and that meant they'd lost. Funny peculiar, that is.

Sunderland: Wonderland

December 1978: I'd met Jim Kriaris, and *Staunch Fan* was now my unofficial calling card. But while I was finding consolation on the soccer periphery, I knew, thanks to Mark's regular aerograms from England, that he was actually living the dream. The return address on his letters was deceptively pastoral – 'High House Farm Cottage, High House Road' in the village of Beetley – but in fact he was in the thick of the action, playing soccer every lunchtime in the British sleet and seeing Manchester United, Arsenal and Liverpool in his fortnightly visits to nearby Norwich City.

It sounded like Mark's family wasn't having a great time of things and, in the worst winter for a decade and a half, a council workers' strike had left snow clogging the streets for days on end. Frozen pipes and leaden skies were a given and the −18C overnight lows were even colder than Ballarat, he assured me unnecessarily. But the day-to-day misery of a sodden, steel-grey winter seemed to act as a thrillingly authentic backdrop to the 1970s English football-fan lifestyle rapidly becoming his second skin. Mark had had his favourite scarf stolen from around his neck after a game, he'd seen stones and bricks thrown, scarves burned, even copped a kicking from Norwich supporters who'd somehow mistaken him for an Arsenal fan. And he'd never sounded as happy.

With Seymour snowed in 100 miles away, the Gunners were gingerly embarking on their latest challenge for the FA Cup. In the era before penalty shoot-outs, a drawn Cup match would be replayed until one team dropped with exhaustion or boredom, and in our first tie, against third-division Sheffield Wednesday, it took *five* games before we beat them 2–0; goals courtesy of stoic young Irish striker Frank Stapleton and the teenage Steve Gatting, whose big-boned big brother was apparently handy with a cricket bat.

Next up – after defeating Notts County – was Nottingham Forest away from home. Forest had just knocked Liverpool off their perch to win their first ever league championship, and two months after playing us they'd claim the European Cup for the first of two consecutive years. In other words, in a matter of weeks Forest would effectively be crowned the best team on the planet; and the year after too. This had all the hallmarks of a thrashing.

Naturally, we were hammered. Everywhere – *ha!* – but on the scoreboard. Stapleton, the granite-faced Dubliner, notched the only goal of the game and we were through to the last eight. Even I had to concede there was now just a chance of the Gunners avenging the Cadet Camp Final.

There was no *League Leader* to report it, never mind anyone to discuss it with, but within a month Arsenal had eased into a second FA Cup final on the trot; Southampton and Wolves meeting their makers. A club could go decades without getting to Wembley and we'd done it twice in succession. Approaching the anniversary of the great Grampians disaster of '78, the Gunners were ninety minutes away (again) from their first trophy on my watch.

One player who wouldn't get to make amends was Supermac. He'd been out injured for months, but with Arsenal on another FA Cup run and the Irish mafia of Stapleton, the Osmond-haired Pat Jennings and the hypnotic Liam Brady making the headlines in *Shoot!* and in the Monday wrap-up in *The Age*, he'd slowly slipped off the radar. With the sketchy information at my disposal, though, I'd assumed Supermac would be back sooner or later, as good as ever.

In fact, the match against Rotherham was the second last of his career. Ineffectual during the Ipswich final he'd had knee surgery straight after the match, and after more failed operations, and almost a year on the sidelines, he'd been forced to admit defeat. Supermac had bagged fifty-five goals in his two full seasons at Highbury, transforming us from a club waiting for the relegation axe to fall into one that might win a trophy before I had grandchildren. Malcolm Macdonald, the greediest, most mutton-chopped, flamboyant, bow-legged goal-scorer of his generation, retired at the age of twenty-nine. Sideburns would be going out of fashion – for a while.

Almost the best piece of news I received in 1979, and the worst Seymour had to endure, was one and the same – he was coming back to Australia. His grandmother had suffered a stroke and Mark, his mum and Jason were on a flight home: she'd make a reasonable recovery, but his British adventure was over. For such a monumental event, it seemed to happen in fast forward. One day Seymour's joyful hooliganism updates, written like he'd weighed anchor there for a lifetime, were trickling through from abroad; the next, Mum was telling me it was Mark on the phone from Ballarat East.

The first conversation we'd had in nearly twelve months was bizarre. 'Orsener, how or yer?' a thickly baritone English voice asked, using my 'Arsenal' nickname as ever. He had to be having a lend with that dense Norfolk twang, but in semi-shock and before I could register a chuckle at his excellent impersonation of a foreigner, I replied nervously, 'Seymour … ah … how's it going?'

I'd imagined our friendship continuing seamlessly, like the last year had been a freeze-frame, but in a matter of minutes I computed the following: (1) Mark's voice had broken, and (2) He sounded like a Pom – really. There was more. He was talking about girls, he was talking about music – 'punk rock', to be precise – and he was pronouncing Norwich 'Norridge'. All with the voice of a man and the accent of an alien. It was great to speak to someone who reminded me so much of Mark, but I still only had his word for it that it was him on the line.

When we met the next day, things were more familiar. He looked basically the same – a bit taller, a bit pimplier – but a couple of stories he told, as we kick-to-kicked in the park at the back of the Kapovics' house, made the hairs on my pudding-bowl haircut stand on end. Mark had fallen in love with a Norridge girl, startling in itself given we'd never acknowledged the existence of the non-FA-Cup-winning sex: then he revealed she was a 'punk'. Norwich was the Alice Springs of England, a town on the east coast marooned 40 or 50 miles from the nearest metropolis, so when Theresa had worn garbage bags rather than sundresses as she went about her daily chores, it was inevitable she'd attract some attention. Mark was impressed. Inspired even.

Diplomat though I was, I don't suppose I hid my surprise at the garbage bags too well. For in late-1970s Ballarat, we did things a bit differently. Molly Meldrum[14] might sneak eight or nine seconds of some spiky band

from the UK onto *Countdown* each week in between
the ELOs, LRBs and Christie Allen but, apart from
that, there was only local radio – 3BA (BAllarat), 3CV
(Central Victoria), and on a clear day 3WM (WiMmera)
– to keep us up to date. That's if you didn't include the
late-night TV show *Breezin'*, hosted by Glenn Ridge, a
chirpy young man with an abundant moustache from
neighbouring Mildura. There – amid a briar patch of
bearded Californians – the Eagles and the Doobie
Brothers dominated the playlist, dotted with an Aussie
band or two that sounded a little like the Eagles and the
Doobie Brothers.

But in May 1979 there were more important issues
at hand than Australia's cultural dependence upon the
sweet sounds of west-coast USA. With Seymour back
we talked till we were red in the face about our – well, his
– recent soccer adventures. Having seen both Arsenal
and United in the flesh, he gave me a blow-by-blow,
brick-by-brick description as I gradually assimilated his
Norfolk accent and the double-bass voice beneath it.
In other years I might have held the upper hand as I
mentioned once, twice – maybe even more – that the
Gunners were in the FA Cup final again. But Mark
wasn't fazed: United were too.

In a way, it only soured his mood. Seymour hated
being here; having fallen in love in England, and *with*
England, an Australian outpost couldn't compete.
Ballarat didn't have punk rock, soccer goals with

permanent nets, or real snow, while St Pat's seemed terminally retarded without the presence of girls. He missed Theresa and, to top things off, before he left the UK he'd had to turn down a ticket to the big game.

If his luck had held out he'd have been there in person – Manchester United v Arsenal at Wembley – maybe being pelted with spit, stones or bricks, perhaps having another favourite United scarf swiped from around his neck as a memento of the event. Instead, he was stuck with the sanitised ABC-TV version of the match of the year, the well-meaning but hopelessly Australian presenters speculating about English football and the FA Cup like palaeontologists at a dig.

Talking about the match was weird too. Back again in our St Pat's uniforms, tramping around the Shed Oval at lunchtime, Mark tried to taunt me, but his heart wasn't in it. We – the English-sounding Australian and the Aussie-accented Englishman – both sensed the anxiety: one of us was going to be miserable soon enough, though admittedly one of us already was. For the sake of the dignity of the loser, we decided to watch the game in our separate homes.

It was hard being around a friend suffering as much as Mark, yet I was desperate for his plight to worsen; just temporarily. We both understood it was nothing personal, but having already suffered one Cup-final loss in tear-stained khaki I couldn't bear the idea of a repeat result on such a huge occasion. While it was a little overdue, at the age of fourteen I'd be watching my first Gunners match live on television.

Arsenal on the radio at Iestyn's place had proven too much for my sensibilities; however, I guess I must have matured – maybe only slightly – because this time round the idea of summoning my powers to will myself to sleep failed to cross my mind. Nevertheless, it was a long Saturday evening, the midnight kick-off an endurance test in itself, with the three of us – Dad, John, home for the weekend, and me – squeezing onto the British-racing-green vinyl couch long before the teams finally walked side by side onto the ground.

I was beginning to shake as the match got underway. But on a bright London afternoon Arsenal started less edgily than I did and had us out of our seats by 12.12 a.m. The Gunners launched an attack with a careering run by Liam Brady, and two seconds later the ball was in the heart of the penalty area. Alan Sunderland – whose mountainous perm put even Brian Kidd's to shame – and Brian Talbot swooped, smacking the ball into the net with a boot apiece: 1–0! And only seventy-eight minutes left.

We were winning in an FA Cup final against Manchester United. The commentator was enthusiastic enough, but didn't seem to understand just how monumental this was, distracted by the peculiar circumstances of the goal. Basically, it was impossible to tell whether Sunderland or Talbot had reached the ball first. It was absurd, and frankly irrelevant, but would the FA Cup be won with a goal shared – half-scored – by two players?

By a quarter to one the answer was no. For most of a drab first half of cat-and-mouse inaction – or thirty minutes of nerve-fraying dental work as observed from a Southern Hemisphere sofa – we held on, and after forty-three minutes Brady shimmied past the tentative United defence again and Frank Stapleton glided a header into the net: 2–0. I spent the half-time break trying to come to grips with it. Teams didn't recover from two goals down to win the FA Cup, the 1953 and 1966 exceptions to the rule – Blackpool and Everton – being pretty much the most remarkable matches in the history of the tournament. It'd take a miracle to beat us now.

Many would later reflect on the dullness of most of the 1979 Cup final, as the first forty minutes of a sun-soaked second half passed with barely a flicker of effective activity from either side. Then with five minutes left, something finally happened – Arsenal substituted David Price for Steve Walford, a midfielder for a defender. The game was dying on its feet: it was brilliant.

Within seconds of Walford coming on to kill off the entertainment, though, something went awry. United lofted the ball aimlessly in from the wing yet again, but this time their blond centre-half Gordon

McQueen stuck out a foot in a congested penalty area, diverting it past a sleepy, suntanned Gunners defence: 2–1. We watched as McQueen ran sternly back towards his own goal for the restart, like the job was barely half – unthinkably, maybe only a third – done. Naturally I had a bad feeling about this. I'd spent forty sweet minutes imagining justice served at last, as an FA Cup final petering out in a worthy 2–0 Gunners win would almost have balanced the ledger for the cruel and unusual Ipswich '78. But McQueen had reminded me that this was *Arsenal*, a team of relegation battlers well capable of losing the unloseable final. Then again, I reassured myself as an optimistic thought crept in among some frenetic nay-saying, the odds were still in our favour. After all, the final whistle was only a matter of seconds – albeit two … hundred … and forty – away.

Unfortunately I'd been right the first time. Two minutes later United's winger Steve Coppell lobbed the ball upfield, somehow finding the feet of his team mate Sammy McIlroy 25 yards out. The situation wasn't desperate yet, but McIlroy slalomed towards goal as a first, then a second Arsenal defender conscientiously slid past him to clear his path. 'McIlroy is through …' the commentator John Motson cried, then repeated, 'McIlroy is THROUGH …' his pitch rising as the nightmare came into focus, the United player's rushed shot trickling goalward. 'And McIlroy …' he paused as it sank in for all concerned '… has done it!!!'

It was 1.45 a.m.; there was silence on the couch. Two goals in a couple of minutes and Manchester United had snatched victory from us: 2–2. A numb 'nnnng …' was all I could muster. One Cup-final defeat, in trying mountainous conditions, had been hard enough to take, but this was something else. In a century of the FA Cup, no team had ever lost a two-goal lead at Wembley in the last four minutes. We were one goal away from an unprecedented, historic disaster.

The match would come to be known as the 'Five-minute Final', for obvious reasons. There was only one more notable event, but it sticks in the memory. Arsenal kicked off and Brady shielded the ball as he loped forward, eating up time to stop a United breakaway for the ever more likely winning goal. He wriggled past a challenge or two and picked out Graham Rix on the left wing. It was Brady to Rix and – following what Uncle Shawn assured us later was Rix's one good cross for the entire season – the United keeper Gary Bailey grasped at thin air and Sunderland steered the ball into the net at the far post. Arsenal 3, Manchester United 2. 'My *word*,' I thought. It was arguably the most dramatic few minutes in FA Cup history. It was unarguably the most unbelievable single thing I'd witnessed in a long and fruitful life. The Cheezels went flying as I threw my arms towards the dark Ballarat sky.

At the age of fourteen, I was virtually without ambition. I imagined, distantly, that I might one day drive a turquoise Ford Mustang with AM/FM radio and alloy wheels and hopefully make a good living doing something fairly easy. Ultimately, though, I had no particular unfulfilled dreams other than through Arsenal FC. And, at 2 a.m., as our stunned captain Pat Rice received the trophy from Prince Charles before a disbelieving sporting world, I realised I now had no particular unfulfilled dreams at all. The Cadet Camp Final had clearly been part of God's master plan, and while I knew it was probably all downhill from here, and I might be driving my grandkids to school in the Mustang, proudly explaining to them the finer points of its AM/FM radio, before we won the FA Cup again, it didn't matter in the slightest.

Half an hour later, the three of us were heading for bed. We'd cleaned up the lounge room – my contribution to suck the air out of a second Coke bottle to make quite sure it was bone dry – and the test pattern was on noiselessly; like the 1979 FA Cup final might never have happened. It already seemed fanciful: Arsenal winning in the most incredible finish in the history of the Cup; ambling to a comfortable win, beaten back by the opposition and looking dead and buried, then stealing it in the last thirty seconds. A matter of minutes earlier, almost the most amazing thing ever to happen to a soccer team had happened to mine. I promised never to complain about anything again – anything at all. Ever.

The Day I Beat Liverpool

From what I could tell, England had changed. Mark had tapes, all sorts of punk stuff compiled from British radio, and they'd become the backdrop to our visits to each other's homes. As I remembered London, there were friendly green parks with hedgehogs and badgers, and Irish singalongs around the piano at reassuring family functions, but Sham 69, the Buzzcocks, UK Subs and others seemed to see it differently.

'Sound of the Suburbs' by the Members was one of my favourites, though the lyrics – replete with sirens screaming at nearby Broadmoor prison, grieving widows who never left the house, and Johnny playing punk rock on his guitar in the dark – were a bit disturbing. Or would have been, if I'd been able to make them out. Punk sounded less like outright shouting the more I listened to it and my family birthday present, Electric Light Orchestra's album, *Discovery* (Mark reckoned it should have been called Disco-Very), was beginning to lose its lustre.

We hadn't quite found a way yet to discuss The

Match. We'd talked about it alright – sort of talked
around it, actually – but while we analysed the Cup final
minute-by-minute at his house and mine, how could I
describe how I felt when Alan Sunderland poked that
majestic cross from Graham Rix into the net to win
the unwinnable, unloseable final? And did Mark really
want to tell me how the FA Cup had rounded off the
worst six weeks he could imagine? But before we'd had
a chance to properly come to grips with our dilemma,
one of us was 12,000 miles away again. Praise the Lord,
this time it was me.

It all happened pretty quickly. Mum, Dad and
I were going on a four-week holiday in England
and Ireland, minus John – with his Higher School
Certificate kicking in – and Anne, who'd decided she
hated overseas. In kids' years, which made a dog year
seem like a fortnight, it was an eternity since I'd been
back and I was curious to see whether punk, with its
garbage-bag fashions and pure anger in general, had
transformed the country I'd thought I knew.

On first sight, England appeared to have
maintained some semblance of order. Three hours or so
after we'd flown into Heathrow, Dad and I were at The
Oval watching the cricket World Cup match between
the West Indies and Pakistan, where anarchy seemed
to have gripped barely two or three hundred people: all
fans of the Windies. In between pithy observations like
'De batsman beginning to see de ball too well – have to

paint it black!' they went berserk with steel drums and trumpets, a bit more joyously than Sham 69 and UK Subs might have led me to anticipate.

Our relatives seemed untouched by the revolution as well. The next day we met up with Uncle Shawn, who, while pleased the Gunners had won a miraculous victory in the Cup, wasted no time in alerting me to the solitary decent cross Rix had managed in the previous twelve months. In the usual mix of lip reading, sign language and other gesticulations we – mainly he – spent a few hours dissecting Arsenal's season, though I didn't get around to confessing to the vital, but unknowing role he'd played in bulking up the later issues of *League Leader*.

Around tea-time I partly turned my attention to *Top of the Pops*, which my cousin Barbara was watching. I hoped the show would be like a video of a Mark compilation tape, but while there was the occasional rowdy track, as with its Australian equivalent *Countdown*, the 'Lay Your Love on Me's and the 'Ring My Bell's ruled the roost. At least until they got to the number-one song: 'Are "Friends" Electric?' by Tubeway Army.

Performed before an audience of bemused thirteen-year-olds, 'Are "Friends" Electric?' was a slough of dispirited synthesisers, the band was veering towards comatose, and the singer – later identified as Gary Numan – looked nervous and I had no idea what he was banging on about. It wafted around for five and a half minutes, with no chorus to speak of, drifting gradually, aimlessly to an end. I realised I might be the first person with an Australian accent ever to have been exposed to this strange sound. Instantly I knew this was my music.

In England, remarkable events seemed to take place around the clock. For instance, within twenty-one days of my 'Are "Friends" Electric?' shock, I'd hold aloft the English championship trophy in Liverpool; be hit on the head with a boot at Wembley; and knock on the front door of the home of an Arsenal defender and be told to push off by his landlady. All up, the stuff of dreams.

Mark and '3 United Supporters, Ballarat' had recorded their psychopathic dislike of Liverpool in *Red 'n' White* and *League Leader*, but I'd never really shared the sentiment. We'd won the FA Cup and I was deeply grateful, but any contract I had with common sense dictated that Arsenal could never win the thirty-odd games out of forty-two required to claim a first-division title. Liverpool inhabited a different corner of the solar system: they were probably the best team in the world – whenever Nottingham Forest weren't. How could you hate someone you couldn't even get near?

So when, during a visit up north to my mum's aunt Peggy and her husband George Evans, Uncle George announced that he'd booked me in for the guided tour of Liverpool's home ground, he was immediately up there with my favourite mother's aunt's husbands of all time.

George Evans – a jaunty bloke unafraid to don the traditional Lancashire flat cap, albeit, perversely, no great soccer fan – and myself fronted at Anfield the next day to discover that a Dutch cricket team had cancelled their booking at the last minute, so there'd be only three of us on the tour. On most occasions, the trophy room might have been a barely penetrable shield of backs and heads with an intermittent flash of something conceivably silver. But today there was room to stride amid an Alpine vista of cups and plaques that I could all but reach out and touch – I could smudge the glass imprisoning them, anyway.

Eventually, the guide pointed something out on a wooden table in the far corner of the room – the first-division championship trophy. I'll say that again (for my own benefit): the first-division championship trophy. I cautiously approached soccer's Shroud of Turin, sitting there in unprotected daylight with red ribbons crowding the handles, a handful of dents only adding to its magical authenticity. Touching the silver, I felt the electricity in my fingertips. For almost a hundred years, the stars of English football had laid hands on the trophy and paraded around Anfield, Old Trafford, Elland Road, even Highbury in prehistoric times, on the greatest days of their lives: Charlie George, Kevin Keegan, Billy Bremner, George Best ...

With his employer having won the trophy four
times in the 1970s, the tour guide wasn't about to get
too misty about it. He scraped sleep, rather than tears,
from his eyes and mentioned that, due to the fixture
list, Liverpool had finished their season early and jetted
off within minutes on their summer break. The upshot
was that I'd hold the trophy before the players who'd
actually won it. In the previous few seasons some of the
Liverpool team had spent as much time with the auld
mug as they had with their girlfriends, but recent signings
like budding Anfield legends Graeme Souness and Alan
Hansen had never been within counties of it. Before
Souness and Hansen; and after Keegan, Bremner, Best
and co. I'm not 100 per cent sure Uncle George fully
understood the import of the moment, but he took the
picture, smiling benevolently but distractedly like *The
Times* crossword aficionado that he was.

Laying hands on the championship trophy was
pretty hard to top, but when you were around Domnick
Taheny, anything was possible. He and I had been born
in the same street in the same month in 1964, and both
we and our parents had been friends. When his mum
arrived in Enfield to take me and Domnick back to
their place for the day, I hadn't seen him for years so I
wasn't sure what to expect. Establishing within about
thirty seconds that he was a Gunners fan, though, and
better still a Gunners fan with connections, I knew I'd
struck it lucky.

By the time we arrived at the Tahenys' outer-suburban Hollywood-glamorous home after a breezy drive in their sparkling new Peugeot 604, I'd additionally concluded that civil unrest in the UK must be fairly localised elsewhere. With the wind swirling through the open windows and down the sunroof as we drove along semi-country lanes I'd taken more oxygen on board than was probably good for me, but I could have sworn I heard Domnick say his family went to the same church as the Gunners defender David O'Leary. Also, that a friend of a friend of his (who'd been blessed with a Christmas card from Frank Stapleton and his girlfriend, if I was getting the whirlwind story straight) happened to know where O'Leary lived.

Domnick's world was hectic and unpredictable, and resistance to it was useless. Back at the Tahenys' place, as he half-watched the horse racing on TV – he had £12 riding on races six to eight – he outlined matter-of-factly that we could pop around any time and see David if we wanted to. Just say the word. And after that, naturally, we'd be off to Wembley.

The David O'Leary episode proved only slightly disappointing. Greeted at the modest two-storey house in question not by a smile and a handshake from an Irish international defender in full Arsenal kit, but by a middle-aged woman with an Irish accent leaning out an upstairs window, we were given fairly short shrift. 'Who told you he lives here?' she asked, with just a trace of irritation, before sending us swiftly on our way. The whole thing lasted about a minute. Convinced, however, that we'd just met David O'Leary's actual landlady, we were well satisfied with our brief outing.

It took two hours across London then to get to Wembley, but the guided tour more or less passed muster. Walking up Wembley Way towards the stadium from Wembley Park underground station, guided by bland street signs, it was all strangely mundane and real. From where the fabled Wembley sat in my imagination, it was almost unsettling that this place really existed, and I was surprised that the stone of the outside walls felt just like a regular old building.

As soon as the tour began, though, surrealism set in. We started in one of the dressing rooms, which contained a huge bath. *Stanley Matthews was photographed here with the FA Cup after Blackpool's win in 1953.* I stared in wonder at the tiles, remembering all the players who'd celebrated here in the annual sudsy tradition after claiming the trophy. *Frank McLintock and the Arsenal team in 1971.* I was getting excited about a bathtub: this tour was going to be really, *really* good.

It was just me and Domnick in the room with half a century of football history. And about a hundred other kids – actually, it was kind of crowded. I squeezed to the front to listen to the guide, who turned out to be witty, incisive, and unafraid to hit a child in the head with a boot. Being at the front I was co-opted into assisting with a couple of demonstrations of soccer's olden days. How hard were the boots they wore in the 1950s? Thunk. *Ow*. Really quite hard. What were the smelling salts like that trainers used to revive injured players? A hundred pairs of eyes looked on as I took a deep breath from the thick glass bottle under my nose. The smell nearly took the legs out from under me. I teetered as everyone laughed a little jealously. Then we headed outside.

After my happy brush with concussion and unconsciousness, we were lined up in two rows in the tunnel at the dressing-room doors; like, say, a couple of teams about to play in an FA Cup final. The green on the horizon was *Wembley*. As we walked out onto the ground – side-by-side just like the Gunners and United and every Cup-final team since 1923 on the exact same stretch of land – a crowd began to roar. Even I was *compos mentis* enough to realise it was a backing tape, but as I strode out there (and some of the kids were chatting, laughing among themselves – I couldn't believe they were wasting the moment) I was still slightly taken aback by the emptiness in the stands.

I was emotionally spent, and the next leg of the tour proved beyond me: climbing the famous thirty-nine steps to hold a trophy in the air as if under the gaze of 100,000 fans. I had to admit I was tempted, but … wasn't it incredibly daggy? So instead I watched ninety-nine others, including a theatrical Domnick, raise a cup excitedly skyward (albeit a scuffed speedway trophy) as they scanned an empty stadium – every one left to imagine, with the tape of the crowd turned off now, what it must be like to hear that roar hitting the London skies.

Baited Breath

A few miles south of Ballarat was Kryal Castle, a moderately tacky tourist attraction ruled by the charismatic King Keith. Owned by a shrewd local businessman also named Keith (possibly the same person), and built in the previous decade from authentic 1960s brick, regrettably it had more rooms than Gothic artefacts to fill them. So the chambers at the far end contained pinball machines and carnival mirrors and, unless I imagined it, a tribute to the pioneering spirit of the town's first residents featuring nineteenth-century mining equipment and kitchenware, most notably a scruffy piece of gauze labelled 'A very old cloth'.

Minding my own business there one Saturday afternoon, sauntering around its cemetery chock-a-block with bawdy rhyming epitaphs, a fully regaled King Keith had seen something in me I'd never seen myself. Plucking me from the crowd, he announced I was to assist him with the Hanging. I looked around in embarrassment and tried to decline, but the King had a persuasive manner and a strong grip. We decided I'd give it a go.

I had no stomach for this, so as the impressively hirsute monarch began the show I was grateful that not too many spectators had noticed the hapless kid stage centre: they were too busy laughing. Although the Whipping of the Wench two hours later held, if anything, even more popular appeal, the 100 cheering onlookers seemed fit to burst as King Keith traded medieval japes with the condemned man (possibly an actor).

At the end of the ceremony, the criminal left to greet St Peter as his body hung limp above the soil of Mount Warrenheip, King Keith elicited a round of applause from the crowd on my behalf – I think my official duties had comprised of handing him the rope and keeping my mouth shut – and rewarded my staunchness with a knighthood. It even came with a certificate.

For some reason I'd been thinking a lot about death. A couple of years on and I appeared to have another opportunity to witness gratuitous human sacrifice within Ballarat & District; in this instance made possible, not by King Keith, but by Mr Kaczkowski. Unfortunately, this time I was it.

Until the week before, I'd been feeling secure. It was great having Mark back, a chance to resume our impenetrable quadrangle small-talk of Andrew Smedleys, Supermacs and Sham 69s, and having an old friend at the sharp end of the St Pat's under-15s didn't hurt. The team was well into its campaign and, despite missing a few games being in the UK, finally I seemed to have found my football niche. Though still scalp to shoulder with most of my team mates and sufficiently slender as to be almost weightless, I could conjure an occasional insightful pass or little shimmy into space and, after years as a Wimmera misfit, at last felt I might be worth a place in the side.

The season was petering to a pleasant close when our coach Mr Kaczkowski – an English immigrant despite circumstantial evidence – called us together after a relaxed Thursday session. This was his cue to announce the starting line-up for the weekend match, but as we encircled him, our clouds of wintry breath creating a smokescreen a few feet above the Shed Oval turf, Mr Kaczkowski had a surprise in store. The St Pat's first XI was depleted due to injuries, he said, so one of us would be needed to step up. There being a decent selection of man-sized, gorilla-breasted players in the under-15s, it didn't seem much of a leap for whoever might get the nod. Then I realised it was my own name being called.

'Me, sir?' I asked with a sickly mixture of terror and disbelief. While I hadn't played badly that season, the 3 or 4 inches I regularly conceded to an under-15 opponent could easily double – or triple, the sky seemed the limit – if I was on a pitch inhabited by grown-ups. Mr Kaczkowski smiled heartily. He actually, preposterously, thought I was the best candidate for the dizzying promotion. 'What about Seymour, sir?' I protested weakly.

In Australia, the round-ball game beloved by the world was considered a pastime for wogs and woofters. From Horsham to Ballarat my eccentric hobby had been tolerated, but at St Pat's, where men were men and Brownlow medallists were old boys, it was understood that playing the foreign sport bordered on dereliction of duty both as a Catholic and an Australian. Wasn't soccer … you know … a bit *womanly*?

Standing on the sidelines as the St Pat's seniors took on Ballarat Grammar I meditated briefly and dismally on the matter. Femininity wasn't what was springing to mind, with the Grammar team more interested in the body-slam than was encouraged by FIFA regulations and their opponents keen to reciprocate. I couldn't see what possible role I could perform in this, other than as bait. On the upside I'd only been enlisted as substitute, but a spate of war wounds seemed inevitable.

Somehow, with a quarter of an hour left, all twenty-two kamikaze pilots remained intact: then the match, and a St Pat's midfielder, took a twist. Crumpling under one of the fusillade of tackles that defined the Grammar style, his game was over. I unzipped my bottle-green tracksuit top with the palm-sized shamrock on the chest, feeling almost as sorry for him as I did for me. This was the kind of pain I shortly expected to be in myself. Ralph Barba, brother of my under-15s colleague Dominic, and debonair star of the firsts – think Marcelo Mastroianni with a stinging shot and an immaculate disco haircut – strolled over as I dropped the tracksuit near the whitewash of the touchline. I was known by a couple of different names and nicknames, so he asked, 'What do you want us to call you, Pat?'

'Most of the under-15s call me "Arsenal",' I suggested, as my stricken team mate limped from the field. Ralph, who was as much a student of the world game as anyone, was evidently horrified at some pallid junior attempting to appropriate one of the biggest names in soccer. 'We'll call you Pat,' he said bluntly.

I jogged nervously onto the ground, my boots hardly making an imprint in the hoof-marks already there. Six inches shorter and 2 stone shy of everyone else on the park, I wondered how I'd even get near the ball. As I formed the thought, the ball appeared at my feet. My career in the seniors – and my life itself, for that matter – was nearly over there and then.

Forty yards from goal, even if I was dripping with nandrolone I'd have been lucky to boot the ball halfway there. Nonetheless the nearest Grammar defender, undistracted by the laws of probability, scythed my waist out from under me and sent me plummeting. The sound was the contents of my lungs hitting the grass.

I wheezed, struggling for breath, as a ruckus erupted overhead. Ralph and the rest of the firsts, who didn't have any reason yet to dislike me, descended like wasps. Someone pushed someone, someone else almost pushed someone else – okay, it wasn't exactly a bloodbath, but I felt proud to be the source of the commotion. All before I'd even touched the ball. Raising myself on an elbow, still puffing like an asthmatic, I saw that the referee had awarded a free kick. Which was nice.

Twenty seconds later, St Pat's were ahead. Ralph lofted the ball deep into Protestant territory, one of our 7-foot strikers nodded it on and another smashed it past the Grammar goalkeeper, who hardly moved: 1–0. My team mates swarmed again, this time in celebration, and, smiling wheezily, I stretched up to pat the scorer on the shoulder as the sweaty organism eased back towards the halfway line. I'd made my only telling contribution to soccer at St Patrick's College.

The following Monday, the shortest kid in Year 10 walked tall. I didn't remember getting a kick, and most of the firsts still wouldn't know who I was if they fell over me, but there was no denying I'd been a key player in a big victory. Seymour gave me the thumbs-up, although we both knew he'd have had a better chance of making an impression other than as team rag doll.

A bruising rite of passage under my belt, there was another issue to address. Mark was leaving again.

It had been on the cards since he'd returned to Ballarat, so it wasn't exactly a bombshell, and at least it was only to Queensland. His dad, who lived in Brisbane and who'd hardly seen Mark since he was six, wanted to get to know his son again. Seymour had mixed feelings, but how bad could it be? Ballarat, especially St Pat's, its Catholic teenage remand centre, was an inexhaustible source of frustration and depression for him, despite my post-FA Cup cheeriness. Rural Victoria just didn't cut it, while Brisbane, though it wasn't exactly London – it wasn't even Norwich – was at least a capital city. And the school he'd be attending was co-educational. Girls. A deal that didn't need clinching got it anyway.

In the midst of all this, the piano made a comeback. Despite the *Jibbidy-F* nightmare of Horsham days, John and I kept on with the lessons and eventually we'd learned proper pieces of music by real composers. I'd become fairly adept at interpreting the works of Miriam Hyde, the uncrowned queen of children's piano, and although, in the age of Bon Scott's AC/DC, songs like 'A Cool Breeze', 'A Merry Game' and 'Gleaming Raindrops' seemed a tad sanitised, thankfully they were nothing that'd get you beaten up.

Mark and I sometimes bashed away on the keyboard, trying to write punk anthems that ended up sounding like Jerry Lee Lewis in oven mitts. The problem wasn't us; it was the piano. After Gary Numan and Tubeway Army all I could picture was synthesisers, while Seymour envisaged deafening, scything guitars. The off-tune ivory racket we made in the lounge room in Ballarat wasn't near enough to be a pale imitation. Still, it helped while away the time before Mark disappeared out the door to Brisbane.

Within weeks, Seymour was gone, and I was walking around the quadrangle, muttering FA Cup commentary incoherently to myself – 'There's a minute left on the clock ... Brady for Arsenal ... right across ... Sunderland!' – to stave off the loneliness. I was sad he'd gone but resigned to it; with John, then Mark, then Mark again leaving me in the lurch, I was getting used to feeling in transit. Much as I'd loved Gary Glitter, his successor in my affections, Gary Numan, seemed to understand me better. On *Top of the Pops* he'd sung plaintively about feeling cold and alone, with the paint peeling off of his walls, and I knew what he meant.

Being fifteen years old was beginning to catch up with me. We'd started career counselling, which chilled me to the core. With Alan Sunderland's winner in the Cup final, I'd fulfilled my life's ambition before puberty had even threatened to make an appearance, and an irrational love of soccer and a vague interest in writing doggerel on the piano didn't seem to add up to much when the clinical, x-ray gaze of a career guidance counsellor was upon me. Amid the joys of a burgeoning spring, I was close to wilting under the pressure.

Perhaps it was a stress-induced hallucination, but while the threat of career guidance shadowed me in the first half of third term, I could have sworn a six-week soccer match broke out. Given its treasonous reputation, an outbreak of the world game at St Pat's hadn't seemed any more likely than a rash of knitting, but one day, inspired by who knows what, fifty or so kids from my year decided to spend lunchtime pounding a soccer ball into submission across a basketball court.

It had quickly evolved into Farmers v City Kids; the Farmers being students who inhabited the rural outposts around Ballarat, the City Kids the sophisticates who didn't. The court – or, rather, two courts end-to-end, encircled by a gladiatorial 15-foot wire fence – was half battlefield, half traffic-jam, as the dozens of us shoehorned into the arena struggled to make meaningful contact with the ball. It devolved into a peculiar hybrid of rugby, wrestling and Rollerball, but, given that there was a goal – two poles holding up the basketball ring – at each end, the ball was spherical and, strictly speaking, you weren't allowed to use your hands, soccer was still the nearest, most accurate title; just about.

It went without saying that the Farmers were a brutal, pagan bunch, and one in a long list of players worth sidestepping was the Head Farmer, Danny Frawley. Later to play 300 AFL games for St Kilda, 'Spud', his nickname throughout his Aussie-rules career, only hinted at the finesse he brought to the soccer pitch. I made sure I stayed on the fringes of the most bone-crunching action – which frequently involved Danny – but even when I scored an own goal from halfway, the ball strenuously shepherded over the goal line by a wall of Farmers, who understood how much more satisfying it was for opponents to score a goal on your behalf, I still loved it.

Naturally, it didn't take long to degenerate into chaos: there'd always been a chance that fifty teenage boys in a cage might turn ugly. Each day the game became more frenetic, the stacks on the mill ever higher, and eventually, in the roving mound of blue-jumpered elbows and barbarous Bata-Scouted[15] feet, no-one seemed to notice whether anyone had brought along a ball or not. I could withstand anything but pain, so of course I bailed out.

I had no regrets, though. There'd been something about hearing the phrase 'You playing soccer at lunchtime?' echoing around the room during Brother Breech's French class that had made my heart leap, regardless of the blood sport they were actually referring to. Maybe I'd been kidding myself about the subtle, balletic pleasures of soccer ever insinuating themselves into the souls of St Pat's Year 10s. But it was nice while it lasted.

Now Boarding

With Mark, John and *League Leader* sadly departed, it had felt like life in Ballarat was grinding to a halt; so when Mum and Dad asked if I wanted to go to boarding school, I watched the word 'Yes' float out of my mouth and I just about meant it. Xavier College would shortly release John unscathed out into the world and, with a vague idea that being a boarder ought to make a man of me – whatever nerve-racking, rib-tickling rituals that might entail – I'd resignedly put my name to the application.

At eight in the morning, the Great Hall at Xavier was nearly empty. This early in the day there was only the occasional knot of three or four boarders, clomping and skating on the polished floorboards between the dorm and the dining room, the sound reverberating in the cavernous Victorian silence. I'd be hunched under the payphone in the corner of the building, and beneath the wooden honour board listing the duxes and captains of Xavier since the Reformation, my entire collection of 20-cent pieces was gradually hoovered down the metal chute as I tried to keep abreast of the final weeks of Arsenal's season.

The chief beneficiaries of a cyclonic few weeks for the Gunners were the major shareholders of Australia's soccer results service. 'Hello … and … welcome … to … the … British … soccer … hotline …' a pleasantly near-comatose voice enunciated as I peered out from under the plastic pod encasing the phone. It was a bit hit and miss. Sometimes you'd ring and they'd still only have the previous day's results, or they might decide that the second and third-division English fixtures were a higher priority than Arsenal's match in the European Cup Winners' Cup and you'd be left smiling apologetically at the other boarders in the queue; some of them maybe wondering why this kid was on the phone four times a week but never spoke to the person at the other end.

Between one thing and another, you had to say it was strange living at a school. No matter how you painted it, there was nothing normal about 100 boys and a couple of dozen priests inhabiting the same slightly gloomy, slightly Gothic housing estate; but it worked fairly well nonetheless. It was a Pacific cruise compared to the stint at the St Pat's gulag that Mark had had to endure – the Xavier Jesuits being, relatively speaking, the groovy uncles of the Catholic education system. In the absence of compulsory confessions and 7 a.m. mid-week masses, and with boarders all but ordered to get out there and mix it with the real people of Melbourne after school and on weekends, first term at Xavier was a blessed relief, given what I'd imagined.

Lights-out in the dormitory was 10.30 p.m., and unless there was a decent pillow fight in the offing the twenty-four of us gradually drifted off beneath a cracked cathedral ceiling. With a transistor sealing my right ear as the radio quietly played EON-FM, hoping to hear 'Ashes to Ashes' or, heaven forbid, 'We Are Glass', I had plenty of time to think. And there was plenty to think about.

For one thing, Arsenal were in the FA Cup semis *again*, while, courtesy of the Five-minute Final, we'd qualified for the European Cup Winners' Cup and progressed to the last four. Early that April, traipsing half-asleep each morning around the nineteenth-century boarders' lockers area, beneath graffiti on a worn slatted roof celebrating former students like 'P Chuck McDonald, Grazier 72–75' and a few dozen others, only one thing troubled me: in the European semi-final, we'd have to play the Italian giants Juventus, while in the FA Cup, we were drawn against ... Liverpool.

After a draw at Highbury, in the second match against Juventus with two minutes to go our substitute Paul Vaessen knocked in a cross: 1–0 and we were in the final. We were a game away from the magnificently ludicrous title of European Cup Winners' Cup winners.

'Juventus … 0 … Arsenal … 1,' announced a voice as animated as an insurance assessor. It was a fantastic, albeit undercover, moment. Almost anywhere in the world and under any circumstances, sport was a collective celebration, but in Australia *not* celebrating was central to the soccer experience. I did an internal lap of honour of the Great Hall, arms akimbo and milking the applause of the crowd in Turin, quietly replacing the receiver and smiling nondescriptly at the next student in line.

This was huge, but the Juventus games were just one thread of a wearying plot. In the FA Cup semi-final, we drew 0–0 with Liverpool, then drew with them again. Thirteen seconds into the second replay, the maxi-permed Alan Sunderland gave us a lead we stubbornly defended for eighty-nine minutes, only for Liverpool's supremely skilful Kenny Dalglish to raise his ugly head. Another draw.

We'd played five semi-finals in nineteen days, been underdogs in all five and hadn't lost one; I was waiting for the cave-in – we were playing *Liverpool*, for pity's sake. It never came. Brian Talbot scored early in the fourth match and this time we hung on. We'd reached a third consecutive FA Cup final – the first team to manage the feat since 1886 – we'd beaten Juventus and Liverpool in very, very slow succession, it was 1 May 1980, and I was a nervous wreck.

Ever the selfless friend, throughout a tortuous

season I'd kept an eye out for Manchester United's results too. For most of the decade United had been as harmless as the Gunners, left in the starting blocks yards behind the league leaders. Come Christmas 1979, though, they were level with Liverpool in top spot. Mark had spent that summer in Ballarat – my last few weeks before boarding school – but despite his team's championship challenge, we hadn't talked much about soccer, only a couple of hours a day maximum.

Seymour had been distracted. Since moving to Queensland he'd embraced the punk ethos down to his studded bootstraps, and while I'd never surpass the shock of his post-pubescent, post-Norwich return to Ballarat, his latest homecoming came close. 'You won't get any stupid haircuts or anything, will you?' his dad had asked after he moved to Brisbane – well, stupid is such a subjective word. While he'd previously been satisfied with a standard '70s chunky style he shared with half the male population under thirty, Mark's hair was now short, spiky and green. *Green.* There was a safety pin in his left ear and he wore a ripped T-shirt with 'Stiff Little Fingers' splashed down the front. His hair was *green*.

At the height of the somewhat conservative reign of Queensland Premier Joh Bjelke-Petersen, where police had unique Joh-given powers such as construing any gathering of more than four people as an unruly mob, Seymour cut quite a figure. Although he looked kind of intimidating – and I saw people cross the six lanes of Sturt Street to avoid a close encounter with Ballarat's first punk – Mark was a self-confessed, self-styled coward. But there was something about the verdant hair, shredded T-shirts and dog collar around his neck that rubbed the Brisbane constabulary up the wrong way. An occasional state-approved thrashing was the inevitable result.

I'd felt I was a long way from the action – thank God – during a lethargic, parched summer in western Victoria. I saw Mark a lot, not least because Mum had an automatic sewing machine; gold bullion in punk terms. He'd come around to talk soccer and music, pursuing his main objective of sewing zips into every piece of clothing in his possession. One item that didn't need much embellishment was his favourite T-shirt, featuring an upside-down crucifix set against a Swastika backdrop, all beneath the word *Destroy* dripping in blood-red ink. I'd never been scared by a shirt before. I was impressed when Mark asked Mum and Dad's permission to wear it at our house: he was fairly committed to offending the world at large, but he would have hated to offend my parents.

John had been home that summer too, and for the first time in a couple of years the three of us had a few weeks to cook up some projects. We never quite got around to it. My brother was off to Melbourne University to study science, I was heading to Xavier to attain manhood, and Mark was covered in zips and preparing for another year at Sunnybank High. Maybe our paths had already diverged too far. We contented ourselves with kicking the ball across the straw-yellow grass of the local park, stockpiling in-jokes about deadpan BTV-6 newsreader Arthur Scuffins and Spod from the Planet Thrrrrn from the *Kenny Everett Video Show*, quietly wondering how life in general and the sci-fi-sounding '1980s' might pan out.

Sometimes life is almost too cruel to record. The most violent act of 1980 wasn't the drawing of blood as Mark tattooed the anarchy symbol on his wrist with a pin and ink; it had to be the merciless unravelling of Arsenal's season. We'd both be left scarred.

The FA Cup final was against West Ham, now stuck in the second division. John and I were back from Melbourne for May holidays and by 11.45 p.m. on Cup final night, we were lined up with Dad, like the jittery back row of a family portrait, in our regular positions on the green couch.

I didn't have a good feeling about this – and rightly so. After sixty-six matches of a never-ending season, the Gunners were asleep on their feet and could hardly muster an attack. The Hammer blow came after thirteen minutes, West Ham's Trevor Brooking heading into the net after his team mate Stuart Pearson – formerly Mark's hero at Manchester United and cover star of the sell-out, debut issue of *Red 'n' White* – had miscued a shot: 1–0. The better team won; one destined to finish twenty-five places lower in the league.

Twelve months earlier to the hour, I'd sucked the last atoms of flavoured oxygen from a 2-litre Coke bottle and wondered how it was that life could be so beautiful: a last-minute winning goal in an FA Cup final will do that to you. This was a different 2 a.m. But while I guessed I'd recover in due course – give it a year or two – the Gunners had four days to do the same. We were up against Valencia of Spain in the European final that Wednesday, if the players could stay awake long enough.

In Ballarat on the Thursday morning, the result was announced unexpectedly on 3BA. The casual ignorance of the local DJ – who wouldn't have known a European Cup Winners' Cup winner if he'd tripped over him in Lydiard Street – stung as much as anything. Valencia had won the cup, he mouthed from the script as my jaw hit the carpet, in the first penalty shoot-out ever in a European club competition. A 0–0 draw, then 5–4 from the spot. And now, the weather forecast for this miserable city.

Two major finals in four days, no goals, two defeats, one 5 feet 1 inch supporter with emotional issues; and the 1979/80 season wasn't done yet. If we finished third in the league, we'd qualify for European competition the next season. With two matches left, we needed to win both.

Back at Xavier a few days later, though, my last Great Hall phone call for the campaign revealed that the red-eyed Gunners had capitulated at Middlesbrough 5–0. I was too deflated to be distraught. Seventy matches, the most ever played by an English club in a season, for nothing. Passing the receiver to the next boarder in line, trying to look like I'd just said goodbye to Mum rather than a dream Cup double and European qualification, I headed silently off to physics. Seventy games.

Injury Time

Boarding school, though painless enough, hadn't even come close to making a man of me: not if aggressively seizing control of your destiny was a requirement. The entire education system seemed geared towards students blessed with the faintest idea what to do with the next five decades of their lives, and having failed, despite the best efforts of the Jesuits, to develop any skills beyond an eidetic recall of FA Cup winners, Arsenal team line-ups, Philips Soccer League attendances and the best players ever whose surname was Macdonald or Brady, the whole experience had been slightly dispiriting.

Mark was way ahead of me. I'd faffed about on the piano a bit in recent years, but my friend had decided he was going to be a *musician*. He and three mates at Sunnybank High had formed a band and, playing to sizeable crowds in Brisbane, supporting such notables as Mental as Anything and Divinyls, were about to release their debut cassette. As far as I could tell from his letters and two or three phone conversations a year, Headcut had become the driving force in Mark's life:

soccer hardly seemed to figure. With the excitement of the day-to-day beginning to supplant anything the distant football world might provide – he was already getting royalty cheques sent to him meant for his namesake in Hunters and Collectors – for the first time since we'd met, United were lagging a distant second, maybe third or fourth, in his affections.

A couple of states away in Victoria, I'd also attained the correct age for outgrowing childhood obsessions. And, to their credit, Arsenal were ensuring I was given every opportunity to come to my senses. Apparently still dazed by the fortnight of Cup-wrenching horror a couple of years earlier, the Gunners were beginning to fray. In the space of a year our two star players had been allowed to walk out the door: Liam Brady to the vanquished but cashed-up Juventus, Frank Stapleton poached by – ironically, *treacherously* – Manchester United. They'd both been at Highbury since they were fifteen.

I felt like my generation was on the way out and there was an air of gloom about the club as we clung to a mid-table spot or thereabouts. It was a throwback to a distant, unsettling past. Going about my daily business of neglecting my university studies as I paced along the almost medieval parapet of Newman College, one of the Catholic campuses of Melbourne University, I realised the next few years might get ugly. Maybe Terry-Mancini, here-comes-relegation ugly.

But my focus was shifting – only slightly – and going to gigs at the university, or across Melbourne at the Seaview Ballroom or the Prince of Wales, clad in red and orange checked shirt, black suit coat, spiky gelled hair and a dab of ghoulish eyeliner, I knew I'd found my niche. I watched *Nicaragua No Pasaran* at the Union Theatre and imbibed its revolutionary message, composed a brutally anti-establishment poem that nearly rhymed for the Newman magazine, and began listening to Joy Division, Bauhaus and The Cure for sheer pleasure. I was getting serious, and the only thing holding me back, threatening my burgeoning counter-cultural credibility was … well …

Anyone with an ounce of common sense would merely have swapped one obsession for another. It was simple: having a rare bootleg of New Order's 'Western Works' demo tape was cool; knowing how many appearances Wilf Rostron had made in the Gunners' first team between 1975 and 1977 less so (seventeen). But I couldn't help myself: after all these years, there was breathing in, there was Arsenal, there was breathing out.

My family and friends aside, the club was the closest thing to a constant in my life. I'd been to six schools and lived in eight houses in five towns and cities in two hemispheres, and nothing much had seemed to stick. But Arsenal had played their home matches at Highbury since before the First World War, a presence as immutable as the laws of science, their red shirts with white sleeves as inevitable as an annual hammering at Liverpool. And while every day I became less English, they remained resolutely, reassuringly so.

By now I was more a fan of the Gunners than I was a citizen of anywhere. Although, thanks to the Socceroos, I'd finally tipped towards Australia. The turning point had come during my high-school days, when the England soccer team toured down under. Frustratingly, with their sole fixture pencilled in for faraway Sydney, making a personal appearance was out of the question, but from a distant vantage point provided by ABC-TV, perversely I had no reason to think I wouldn't be fervently supporting both countries.

England would face the Socceroos with a reserve line-up, fielding youngsters such as future national coach Glenn Hoddle and captain-to-be Bryan Robson, as well as fringe players like the tireless Brian Talbot and frizzy Alan Sunderland, the Arsenal duo who'd nearly shared a goal in the Five-minute Final. Meanwhile Australia was at full-strength; insofar as the term applied to a team of part-timers who'd cadged a few days off work to fulfil the fixture.

Naturally, the other boarders wanted to watch the Saturday night movie rather than a soccer match featuring two-dozen blokes they'd never heard of, so I knew I'd have to improvise. One of the classrooms at the far end of the school, pretty much a couple of kilometres away, had a TV on wheels, and I borrowed the keys from one of the priests. With thirty-five vacant desks for company, only slightly freezing on the last Saturday night before winter in an unheated, spookily half-lit room, I watched the Socceroos fall a couple of goals behind before I'd even found a comfortable sitting position.

It was an historic event – the first ever full international between the two nations – and after Hoddle and Paul Mariner, Ipswich's FA Cup-winning striker, had tucked goals away inside the opening twenty or so minutes, a sobering loss for the Aussies was on the cards. Then something happened: I realised I was horrified at the prospect. Improbably, I really wanted Australia to win – leading to a likely England defeat. Which, I was startled to discover, was more or less okay by me.

The England team was fizzing the passes around and belting the shots in at Socceroos goalkeeper Greg Woodhouse, but the home side kept the professionals at bay till half-time. Then with an inspired substitution, Peter Sharne, the nimble winger from PSL club Marconi, entered the Sydney Cricket Ground arena. He was everywhere, giving Leeds United's Trevor Cherry – who possibly *didn't* work in a warehouse or a factory four days a week – a miserable time. With three minutes left, Sharne was fouled in the penalty area, Gary Cole smacked home the spot-kick, and the final score of

2–1 left honour satisfied, and me all but sporting a new nationality.

In my mid-teens, I'd made peace with my demons. I was capable of barracking for this country I'd lived in for a decade, even against my homeland; whatever homeland meant. You couldn't say it made me Australian, but at least I was in the ball park. And though it didn't quite click at the time – being more intent on blindly feeling my way in the dark from the outpost classroom through a maze of brick back to the Year 11 dormitory – the antipodean accent I'd dragged around since I was seven or eight would finally begin to sit more easily.

I'd always needed something from England, but now maybe not. By 1984, my third year of sleepwalking through a Bachelor of Arts degree, though the UK retained its air of excitement I remembered it as much for what had changed as for what was still intact. During my last visit five years before, I'd noticed the phasing out of *Doctor Who* police boxes, the absence of *Captain Scarlet* from afternoon television, and with only the occasional 1960s Vauxhall, Wolseley or Sunbeam chugging rustily past, there hadn't been too many reminders of the landscape I'd left behind as a child. All up, a fair percentage of the artefacts I'd come to associate with Britain had gone the way of black-and-white TV.

The only ghost of pure Englishness I could detect

was in my inability to embrace Allan Border, Dirk
Wellham and Kepler Wessels as true compatriots. I
understood this was attributable to the spectre of John
Edrich and the frequently hospitalised Spirits of '75, but
despite the brave undertakings of Mr Edrich, Dennis
Amiss and his cohorts, Firebrace Street in Horsham,
where Speedos were compulsory three months a year,
felt much more like home than football-loving, flip-flop
wearing, cockney-dotted Chase Road, London N14.

On the last weekend that February, I severed my
last contractual links with a Catholic childhood, leaving
the barb-wired confines of Newman College to move
into student accommodation in Lygon Street, Carlton,
opposite the 14-storey Housing Commission flats; an
old terrace house that creaked every time a self-penned
poem was Blu-Tacked to the corridor wall.

I hauled my belongings through the iron gate
and up the mountain of front steps inside the door,
dragging them into my bedroom, a narrow cubby hole
between the living room and kitchen. With my suitcases
and plastic bags strewn across the bear-brown carpet,
I gazed dreamily out the muddy, curtainless windows
onto our little concrete garden.

Despite fertile ground for contemplation, there
still wasn't much more on my mind than there'd been
a decade and a half, a generation, and a nationality
earlier. We were playing Nottingham Forest at the City
Ground that night, a chance to bullet from sixteenth

to fourteenth in the league. And with a few more wins, maybe a decent unbeaten run, perhaps a hefty slice of luck here and there, we'd be up in the top eight again. With or without Stapleton, Brady and Supermac.

I began to unpack my suitcases and bags – the Cure, Joy Division, Japan and MEO 245 albums and 12-inch singles slowly stacked in a brown-skirted, whitewalled corner – as I did my weekly three-points-a-win arithmetic. A draw might get us to fifteenth, if Aston Villa lost to Ipswich and Leicester didn't beat Sunderland. We hadn't won any of our last five, but a draw against Villa the previous week was more promising. Graham Rix had scored twice in two games, which suggested he was coming into a bit of form. And our new signing, the Bono-lookalike Charlie Nicholas, might yet come good. Those couple of goals he'd got against Tottenham on Boxing Day augured well. I was only slightly distracted by the metallic rhythm track of a No. 1 tram out on Lygon Street heading for East Coburg. Go Gunners.

Epilogue

The crowd was a choppy sea of red, white and blue, chanting fans draped Chilean flags over their heads to shield themselves from the endless rain, and the South Americans won at a canter – the 1–0 score line no real indication. The celebrations spilt into the traffic outside, the carnival continuing long and raucously after the supporters had left the stadium. It was a great night to be in Santiago. It was a shame we were all in Melbourne.

The Chilean national team was touring down under and in a way it was just like old times. A foreign side comes to Australia, swathes of the crowd barrack against the Socceroos and go home happy after hammering the modest local opposition, the result barely scraping into page seven of the sports section (despite a majestic match report). Ten weeks earlier the Australians had played Iran a few hundred metres away at the MCG as half the country looked on. Now, with the stuffing knocked out of Aussie soccer, four more years on the sidelines till we'd get to lose in the qualifiers again, the game was back where it belonged: like an apparition of Our Lady, visible only to the devout.

There were 12,000 people at Olympic Park – a slight 80 per cent downturn from the MCG fixture – and 10,000 of them, the 10,000 muttering anything above a mournful whisper, had a distinctly Andean look. The couple of thousand Australian fans, damp and despondent, were there under sufferance, every kick reminding them of Iran and how much they hated supporting the Socceroos. In the press box the mood was similar, although having shed the part-time AFL and cricket correspondents since the World Cup match, at least the few of us left could commiserate in peace. After the game, the media chose Australia's official man of the match. I voted for the enigmatic Gabriel Mendez, prompting a quiet chuckle around the room. To general amazement, Mendez took home the award. It was as if I'd handpicked the winner, like nobody had bothered to cast a vote for anyone else. It was a far cry from Iran.

If there'd been a more miserable evening to be a fan of Australian soccer, no-one could remember it. Yet, things had changed. For a couple of weeks the previous November, people – mythical 'mainstream Australians' – had been captivated by the world game, and those at the Iran match, like Test cricketers and Australian-rules players who'd seen plenty of packed houses at the old stadium, said they'd rarely heard a crowd like it. All I'd wanted since I was nine was for soccer to matter to people around me, and amid a lost opportunity – the Socceroos 'choking', Venables getting the tactics wrong, or, pick a defender, finding a scapegoat for Iran's second goal – I'd apparently got my wish. Albeit fairly well disguised as ignominious failure.

It was still bucketing down as I was leaving the stadium, but, grim evening or not, from under my umbrella there was a cosy familiarity to the scene. I'd been to dozens of matches at Olympic Park, the wind-buffeted, treeless plain of Australian sport that frostbitten soccer fans swore boasted an icy microclimate all its own. I'd been feted by the Footscray JUST team in one of its dressing rooms, scored the autographs there of footballers as illustrious as New York Cosmos reserve goalkeeper Hubert Birkenmeier, even helped SBS-TV's Les Murray conduct an interview – anchoring a spotlight with my feet in a typical Force-10 gale (Adelaide City's million-pound English guest-player Justin Fashanu, 16 July 1980); only a cold-hearted man could turn his back on a place like this.

Over the years, I'd looked on as the Socceroos had lost to Fiji, Tottenham Hotspur's reserves and an Italian Army XI, but I guess by now we were stuck with each other. After all, from Gary Glitter to Gary Numan, from North Melbourne FC to Arsenal FC, I'd always been drawn to the unloved and the unlikeable.

I'd never really needed anyone other than John and Mark, sometimes Dad and Uncle Shawn, on board to get full value for my soccer experiences. Another eighteen million Aussies would only be a bonus.

Iran was a shame, I concluded as I approached a taxi rank, but at least Australia had played brilliantly that night; even Socceroos-sceptic George Best might have been impressed. And the fact that our best players were good enough now to represent clubs like Leeds, Aston Villa and Southampton, keeping actual English players out of the local teams, was a great sign. So was our ability to attract a coach of Venables' stature and entice a massive crowd to a World Cup qualifier. With all that in place, I pondered, listening to the singing and drumming of the damp but delirious Chilean fans echo from across the street, surely Australia had to break through to reach the finals sooner or later. Then again, having anticipated just such a thing since John's and my scouting mission for the Aussies at Enfield v Kuwait back in 1977, I thought I might leave the Mystic Meg right there. Thinking better, as well, of inflicting a Socceroos monologue on an unsuspecting cab driver despite the monsoon beginning to envelop Olympic Park, I steered past the taxis and towards the city. It was only a short walk through the downpour to Flinders Street station.

Endnotes

1.   A 1970s and '80s children's semi-educational TV program hosted by brainy, hirsute men in cardigans. Incandescent scientific experiments and improbable futuristic inventions were guaranteed.

2.   Moderately popular lollies, or sweets, of the time. On the downside they were pink; on the upside, they were kind of shaped like a cigarette and you could pretend to smoke them. As a last resort.

3.   Marchants lemonade. A local brand. You'd only buy it if the tuck shop had run out of Fanta.

4.   The Victorian Football League, planet Earth's finest exposition of Australian Rules football. Front and back-page coverage in Melbourne, the Wimmera and all points in-between was frequent.

5.   A back-garden toy you could hang off a few feet from the ground and spin around on till you felt sick. Original intended use: a height-adjustable, rotary washing line.

6.   A big story at the time, on the TV news every night for months, involving the Australian government, a Pakistani businessman with dark glasses, and money being borrowed or something. Not understood by anyone at my school.

7.   This being the battle, fought mainly in the playgrounds of primary schools across Australia, between fans of the genial pop music of Sherbet (signature song: 'How-ow-ow-zat') and the edgier, scarier Skyhooks. I leant towards Sherbet.

8.   Long-serving Australian Prime Minister who said of Her

Majesty Elizabeth II in 1963, 'I did but see her passing by, and yet I love her till I die.' How very true.

9. Local TV pop music show, hosted by the eccentric, cowboy-hatted Ian 'Molly' Meldrum.

10. A Labor Prime Minister in the 1970s. Ambitious, socially progressive, he called colleagues 'comrade': he was viewed with suspicion in country towns.

11. In the late 1980s, a cashed-up national Aussie Rules competition – hence the 'A' in 'AFL' – had replaced the state-based Victorian Football League.

12. Awarded to the Victorian Football League best-and-fairest Australian Rules footballer of the year. A mouthful, but prestigious like a knighthood wished it was.

13. Venerated Australian actor blessed with a rich, resonant voice. He played Pontius Pilate in *Ben-Hur*. Yes, *Ben-Hur!*

14. Ian 'Molly' Meldrum: the aforementioned cowboy-hatted TV music-show host.

15. Bata Scouts being a type of boy's school shoe. They had a compass in the sole; hence the best shoe ever.

About the Author

Patrick Mangan was born in north London and his family migrated to Australia when he was five. In the mid-1990s, he became editor of *Soccer Australia* magazine and later worked as the soccer reporter for *The Sunday Age* and *The Age*. Patrick is beginning to accept that he will never play for Arsenal. But he hasn't yet given up on the Socceroos.